Open Reference Architecture for Security and Privacy Documentation

Release 2019-Q1

Maikel Mardjan & Asim Jahan

Mar 31, 2019

CONTENTS

This reference architecture is built around information that helps you creating security or privacy architectures. This reference architecture is created to improve security and privacy designs in general. In our opinion it is time to stop reinventing the wheel when it comes down to creating architectures and designs for security and privacy solutions.

The reference architecture is not just another security book. Since libraries and book stores are filled with decent books on security and privacy we wanted to create a book that is all about reuse.

FOREWORD

Note: We are continuously working on updates on this publication. Join the team and contribute too! The latest version of this publication is always online at https://security-and-privacy-reference-architecture. readthedocs.io

---

Freedom is, was and will always remain important. This applies to our physical world as well as our digital world. To maintain our freedom we need protection and good IT security. Good security brings freedom the way you want and enables you to exchange information without censorship or monitoring. Your secret information and your communication belongs to you. So take measurements to make is yours again.

Privacy needs solid security to start with, but if you value your own freedom, you should respect your customers freedom too. So make sure your users can trust you. So respect their privacy by using tangible privacy measurements by design principles when creating new solutions.

Good security and privacy do not have to be endlessly expensive. It all starts with good architecture and a solid design. This reference architecture gives you a head start for creating your specific security and privacy designs. You can use the proposed security and privacy principles and the sample requirements to start with. Furthermore you can use or start with security models we present in this reference architecture as well. Also a list of example security system building blocks is presented. Since open source solutions can be valuable to lower security risks and reduce cost in your organization all presented solutions in this reference architecture are open source. This book also presents a list of criteria to evaluate the quality of OSS security and privacy solutions is.

Good privacy and security is difficult and complex. Making use of information presented in this book assures you do not have to reinvent the wheel so to say. Good security and privacy design for information systems is important. So do not lose your valuable time on trivial aspects. You need your time to solve the security and privacy challenges for your unique situation!

Good protection for our privacy is getting more and more difficult and expensive. In our opinion freedom requires very strong privacy protection assurances. We do not live a world where cyber security is always at a normal (low) risk level. You need more protection measurements by default to protect your core information assets like personal and business information and your valuable privacy data records. We still have a long way to go. But using solutions provided in this reference architecture will lower your security and privacy risks.

For privacy and security we need strong governance institutes that set rules to keep our (online) freedom.

If you want to help to remain freedom and want a more secure world, consider to support e.g. The Electronic Frontier Foundation (https: //www.eff.org), a non-profit organization defending civil liberties in the digital world. Or support a similar local non-profit organization in your country.

INTRODUCTION

In our opinion security is a process, not a destination to arrive at. Good security design and implementation takes time, patience and hard work to achieve and maintain. You should always start with the basics by creating an architecture or overall design. As security and privacy will always be one of the most important subjects within IT the importance of good security and privacy will keep growing since companies will be even more depending on IT. Also the influence of IT will go deeper into our lives. Next to safety security and privacy will become more important when we realize the potential risks that come with new IT technologies.

This reference architecture is created to improve security and privacy designs in general. In our opinion it is time to stop reinventing the wheel when it comes down to creating architectures and designs for security and privacy solutions.

This reference architecture is not just another security book. Since libraries and book stores are filled with decent books on security and privacy we wanted to create a book that is all about reuse. There are two main pillars that drive this publication:

- Enabling reuse for companies of all sizes worldwide in order to design security and privacy solutions.

- Creating an open reference architecture that enables collaboration and improvement in an easy way.

This reference architecture aims to enable you to create better and faster security and privacy solutions by reusing the content provided in this publication. And to encourage collaboration on this publication we created this reference architecture under an open license. We have chosen to use the Creative Commons Attribution-ShareAlike 4.0 International

(CC BY-SA 4.0) license. We know you like credit if you contribute to a publication. If you contribute you will of course be mentioned in all updates of this publication that follow. And since it is a true open license, your rights regarding this publication are no different than ours or other contributors.

To summarize this publication is an open reference architecture aiming to help you to design better and more secure systems in less time and with less cost.

2.0.1 Why another reference architecture

Open publications for IT security and privacy are still rare. Despite the great work of the OWASP foundation many IT security organizations are not that open.

When you create a new medicine that can and will save millions of human lives it is not only ethical but also a moral right that people can use it. Science is there so we can build on each other's ideas.

This means progress for all. We all win. Within the field of software coding Open Source (OSS/FOSS) is becoming the new de facto model. Why create something anew that you already have created?

Within the field of security consultancy and security architecture Open is not (yet) the de facto standard. Of course some key assets as passwords or personal data should never be accessible. But creating security architectures and security designs is by many positioned as an art. That is strange of course. If you need a new color on your wall you do not call an artist, but a painter. The same goes for security: go for a proven open solution that has been used before. All solutions are of course mostly always context specific. No organization is the same. But that does not mean that every aspect for your architecture, and design should be new. We all use standard solutions where possible. Reuse of architecture and design is rare at the least. This reference architecture is aimed at enabling reuse of parts that are needed in every security architecture and design. That means less art, but the puzzle that remains is more interesting to solve. Since this is the real context related problem!

Availability of good references with solid reusable information makes creating security architectures easier and more fun. Easier because when you have a good security reference architecture you do not need various books to find out what already good proven parts for your architecture could be. More fun because you have more time to figure out what the best solution for your unique security challenge is. And we see thinking and resolving real security issues as fun. Minimizing security and privacy risks is always unique and context depended. E.g. unique stakeholders, different security control system (organization) and a different way of dealing with risks.

2.0.2 Why security and privacy

Privacy is getting more and more important. New technologies make our lives better but put our freedom and privacy under pressure. Terrorist and (cyber) criminals can be more easily detected by analyzing large amounts of data. Also 'diseases' can be better cured using more data of more people.

Currently great improvements come at a large price: Big data analytics systems are going over your user data and user data traces (e.g. mouse movements in web pages, location data) multiple times a day. Companies know better what you need, think and eat tomorrow than you. Your location is continuously being tracked, due to all the communication devices you use. Using public transport cannot be done anonymously anymore while cars are full of track and tracing technology.

When privacy is designed first just as security we should have less concern on security and privacy hacks. Also if more IT designs are open and published under an open license chances of mistakes in architecture and design will be less. Partly due to pressure of openness but also since more experts can contribute to lower security and privacy risks concerned with public or private systems. Of course: Transparency of governmental systems will be a (very) long way. Companies however see advantages of open solutions more and more. Using open solutions, open business models and open source software for IT. A large number of companies exist that benefit from using open designs along with open source software.

Many new technology companies are successful due to the fact that they promote open (FOSS) solutions. E.g. Companies like Automattic (https://automattic.com/), Acquia (https://www.acquia.com/) or IMatix (http://www.imatix.com/) are all very successful due to a true GPL OSS policy.

We know that privacy can be regarded as something totally different than security. This is why we had some resistance with combining a reference architecture for security with privacy 'things'. But our research showed that:

- Privacy has many relations with security. Many problems are similar.

- Privacy aspects are by far not yet taken serious into architectures and design the way they should be. It took decades and billion dollar (or euro) campaigns before security aspects were taken more seriously into account. And yet security is still difficult due the fact that doing it right gives no direct business value. Doing it wrong always means a true disaster for your business. And he same goes for privacy.

- Security and privacy are interrelated. Without security there is no privacy! Never.

Since privacy and security are very much interrelated both aspects will be outlined in this reference architecture.

2.0.3 Advantage of using this reference architecture

A good reference architecture saves time in many ways:

- You can create a solution architecture based on it for your specific situation.

- It enables you to speed up the process of creating a specific solution.

- It contains valuable content and general background information which can be used, reused or referred to.

Information security architecture is an abstraction of a design that identifies and describes where and how security controls are used. It also identifies and describes the location and sensitivity of both user and application data.

This open reference security architecture aims to help you create your context specific architecture faster and with higher quality.

This reference architecture is designed to assist and guide architects, security designers and developers to make better decisions and to reuse quality architecture knowledge regarding cyber security aspects.

The purpose of this document is to reuse good security principles, requirements and design patterns to save precious time and budgets. Since security by obscurity is in general not a good practice, we also provide a list of OSS security software products.

Systems built with tough privacy rules will not always guarantee that information including valuable privacy content is secure. Since security never is nor can be perfect a very secure system will always contain risks concerning privacy.

2.0.4 Who should use this reference architecture

The target audience for this reference architecture are security experts and companies who can see the benefit of reuse and using open source security building blocks. Specifically all business owners, security architects, security designers, asset owners, software developers, system administrators and (end) users who have a role in reducing security risks.

2.0.5 Scope of this reference architecture

Not all aspects of security and privacy can and should be outlined in a reference architecture. This reference architecture is not about teaching what security and privacy is. This reference architecture is not about providing detailed technical information on solutions that come across.

This reference architecture is also not a lecture book on how to design the perfect security solution architecture. There are many resources (books, courses, foundations) that will teach you the benefits of creating an (enterprise) architecture and how you can embed architecture into your agile way of working. Be aware of course that an agile way of creating new products, systems or software gives some tension regarding security and privacy aspects. It is difficult to add security and privacy aspects at a later point if not done correctly from the start. So use new trends whenever possible. But if you were to design 'A human mission to Mars' important aspects like security and safety cannot wait till later.

Since you are reading this reference architecture, we assume you are already aware of the complex field of security and privacy. Very detailed books, papers and studies exist for learning what security and privacy really is. So this reference architecture will not give you in depth detailed background information on all security and privacy aspects. Not from an organization point of view and certainly not from an IT point of view.

The scope and aim of this open security architecture is to enable you to create better and faster security solution architectures and designs using open reusable building blocks and standards. Within the scope of this reference architecture are:

- Security solution aspects, e.g. models, that must, should or could be reused in a security or privacy solution architecture.

- Information that can be reused in an easy way in your context specific security/privacy solutions. E.g. security and privacy principles.

- Criteria aspects you can reuse when selecting security solutions for your solution architecture.

- (Sample) Security/Privacy Solution Building Blocks that are created for reuse. These SBB's serve as example to give you a more in depth overview of possibilities you are maybe not familiar with.

Within this reference architecture we will focus on the following subjects that you should face when creating a security or privacy solution:

- Principles: We will provide a reusable list of security and privacy principles. Since this open security and privacy reference architecture has an Open approach we encourage you to add your principles to the open data source we created to help others from reinventing the wheel again and by doing so they save time.

- Solution Building Blocks: We provide a list of solid reusable security and privacy tools and building blocks. Of course all tools and building blocks are open source. One core principle is that good security should be open. Within this eBook a detailed outline is given on the question if extra risks factors are involved in using open source solutions.

- Reusable architecture and design patterns for security and privacy problems. During the architecture and design phase threat models are constructed. This document contains generic threat models, since these are reusable. That can be improved when the model is made publicly available.

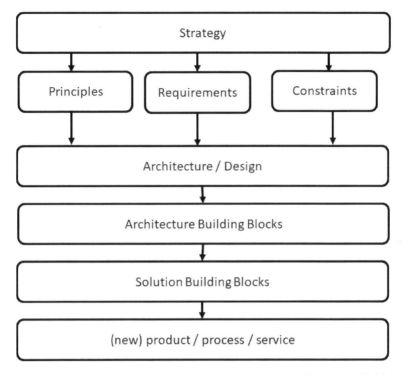

Many aspects regarding security and privacy our not in scope of this reference architecture. The clear and only focus is on providing open content that makes creating solutions for common security and privacy challenges simpler.

2.0.6 What about security patterns?

In system design, coding and architecture you should strive to reuse pre-defined patterns. A pattern is a reusable way to solve a standardized problem. This can be in software code, design or an organization problem.

Good patterns within the security and privacy field are rare. We did research on available reusable patterns that can help creating security or privacy solutions faster. Our findings are:

- Good described reusable security and privacy solution patterns are rare.

- Reusable architecture and design patterns for security and privacy problems are scarce. Most relevant patterns are vendor specific, so are targeted to the solution building block reuse aspects.

- Use of patterns can increase complexity. Understanding pattern language and semantics is important before being able to judge if your chosen pattern applies to the unique challenge that must be solved. Since libraries are written on generic problem solving methods (note: the golden book is still not found) some precaution using patterns is very healthy!

- Developing usable patterns (also in a collaborative way) for a reference architecture takes up a lot of time while the practical use (or reuse) in a solution architecture is often limited.

We hope good developed patterns for dealing with typical security and privacy problems will be developed in future. Also we hope these patterns will be developed in an open collaborative way and published under an open license so everyone can benefit and participate. Some good attempts have been done, so maybe time for a new OWASP project to give it a boost.

Currently we think that when you write a good solution architecture in which you describe your problem clearly will help to create a library of reusable solution patterns for security and privacy. One import constraint is that your solution architecture should be published under an open license somewhere on the internet. In this way every organization, security designer can benefit. Some governments already publish their architecture documents under an open license (CC) on the internet. This is a great way for governments to align better with society. Everyone can see how complex digital information systems become and can suggest improvements. Detailed configuration information is not needed to judge the risks of security or privacy vulnerabilities. Companies worldwide are still very anxious to benefit from the possibilities that a more open transparent company (using open licensing) can give.

2.0.7 How this reference architecture is structured

This reference architecture is built around information that helps you creating security or privacy solution architectures.

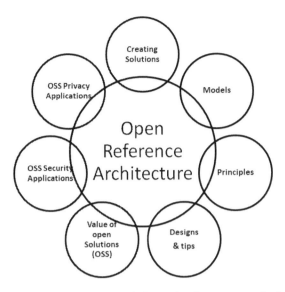

It is also built to give you reusable information in an easy to find way. The next chapter ('Security Models') deals with models, attack vectors and information that helps you create the threat model you need to develop in your solution architecture.

The chapter 'Security and Privacy Principles' presents solid security and privacy principles. Focus is on use and reuse. The chapter 'Using Open Source for security and privacy protection' outlines facts to demystify common fads regarding use of Open Source and security and privacy products. This chapter outlines how to evaluate OSS Solution Building Blocks for security and privacy applications. The chapter 'Open Source Security and Privacy products' presents a list of great OSS solutions available to be incorporated into your security or privacy solution or just to take a look at.

The appendixes will give you information on reference used, as well as information on how you can contribute with the next version of this reference architecture.

CREATING A SOLUTION

This section outlines a clear and simple way to create your security and privacy solution.

3.0.1 The steps

To create a sustainable solution for security & privacy issues the best start is to create a solution architecture. Since an architecture itself does not protect you but an good solution architecture reduces costs, time and lowers risks. This because in an architecture the emphasis is not only on the IT part and technical solutions but also on embedding solutions into your organisation and processes.

The perfect solution to reduce security and privacy risks to zero does not exist. An solution architecture helps in the process of optimizing and controlling your risks.

A good way to really speed up creating your solution architecture is of course to use this reference architecture as basis. This open reference architecture is created to make security & privacy architectures better and help within the process of creation.

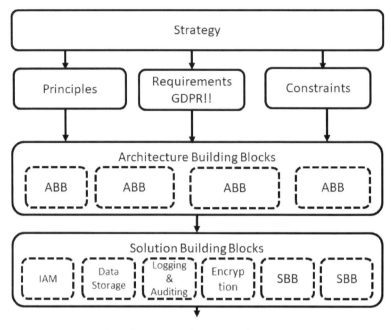

(new) product / process / service

Creating security a security or privacy solution architecture consists of the following high level steps:

- Dive in the business strategy and organization;

- Gather security and privacy principles and requirements;

- Determine important constraints that apply to your architecture or design. There are always constraints, e.g. time, budget, subject matter experts available etc.

- Derive the architecture building blocks from your architecture or design. Architecture building blocks help you to scope your solution. Using architecture building blocks gives a clear view on (new) integration aspects and where completely new solutions fit in the total IT landscape.

- Select (or create, buy) the new Solution Building Blocks. Prerequisite is of course that the functionality and technical constrains must be clear. Often prerequisites are derived from the previous design step.

So first create architecture building blocks that will form the basis of your solution. The last stop to find solution building blocks that will implement your specific problem (ABBs) that match your specific requirements, principles and constrains.

3.0.2 OSS Security and Privacy SBB Selection

When you are aware of the advantages and disadvantages of using open source building blocks for your security architecture or design, this reference architecture provides an up-to-date overview of really great open source security solutions.

A known difficult taks is to select (or create) solution building blocks that covers the needed functionality. Of course you should always start with principles, requirements and constraints first. And remember: No single tool will fit all use cases. So select the right tool for the right job.

To give some guidance on selecting products to lower risks on security and privacy a conceptual model can be usefull. The key of a usefull conceptual model is that a seperation is made between the needs (requirements) and the solution ('the how') is clear.

3.0.3 Architecture view of Security Applications

The number of OSS security applications available is over overwhelming. Using the following conceptual topology can help with arranging functional to product mapping needs:

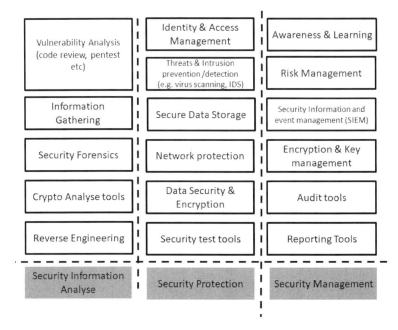

For every security or privacy function or service needed you should look serious at using open transparent reusable solutions. So Open Source. Of course many vendors provide good solid security products for specific use cases. But when you feel you need a trivial security or privacy service, there is almost always a working and maintained OSS application available. When using OSS solutions, you have have a large choice of companies that deliver maintenance and support on this application on commercial bases.

3.0.4 Architecture view of Privacy Applications

Besides strong security measurements strong encryption is hard to accomplish. Especially online and when you do not use FOSS software in combination with open hardware that you can really trust! However due to the growing importance privacy the number of FOSS tools available is increasing. An framework for putting privacy Architecture Building Blocks on a map:

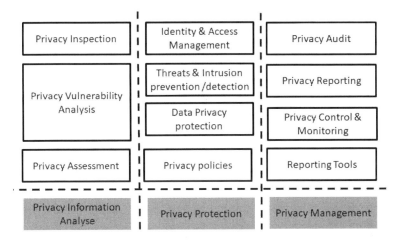

Using this privacy ABBs you can select OSS Solution Building Blocks that match your requirements. And remember: No single (OSS or commercial) is perfect. A tool alone will never be enough. So make sure you have a good balance between tool support and a good privacy and/or security organization to manage risks.

FOUR

SECURITY AND PRIVACY MODELS

4.0.1 Introduction

The essence of information security is to protect information. It is just that simple. So whenever possible do not make it more complicated than needed. Complexity for cyber security and privacy arise when information needs to be shared or must be made accessible by some digital device. The world where information was only available in physical archives is long gone. The focus from physical information security is shifted to cyber information security. But be aware: Crucial principles of centuries of physical information protection are still valuable today. Especially principles related to the intangible soft issues when information is shared. Ever wondered how some organizations managed to keep their valuable information secret for many decades?

Information protection is needed against unauthorized access, use, disclosure, modification or destruction. That means several security measures are needed to protect information from unauthorized viewers. Measures can be implemented by procedural, physical or with complex IT tools. But before classifying and creating or finding good measures it is essential that the problem field is made clear.

Creating effective solutions for information security problems can be done by creating a model of the problem situation. Within a model all elements that relate with the problem situation are brought together to study effective solutions. Without going into detail on system science or problem solving theory: in general systems consist of sub-systems, objects, functions or processes, and activities or tasks.

The key in creating a good model to solve a specific information security problem is to model the problem, not the complete system with all elements. This because modelling the world completely is ineffective, time consuming and it does not give a direct answer to solve a problem situation. It is far better to start with a small model of a problem and create extensions on this model if needed.

The field of modelling problem situations to solve information security problems is not new. Many models in literature exist. Reusing a good model can save you time and safeguards you from making mistakes. A prerequisite is that you start with a good model that can be trusted and is intensively reviewed by large numbers of subject matter experts.

There are many good security models that can assist in creating a solution architecture to solve a specific security problem for an organization. Mind that a model can be expressed in many different forms. E.g.:

- One or more images;

- Text;

- Software model

Within the field of modelling a distinction can be made between 'hard' and 'soft' models. Hard models are often mathematical (risk) models whereas soft models are more quality based models. Since using hard models often gives a false sense of reliability and requires full insight of all assumptions made it is more productive to reuse soft security and privacy models. When creating solution architecture, you need:

- A threat model (what are the threats your solution gives protection against)

- Insight in commonly used attack vectors. This means you need to have some view on the attack vectors used in the use case?

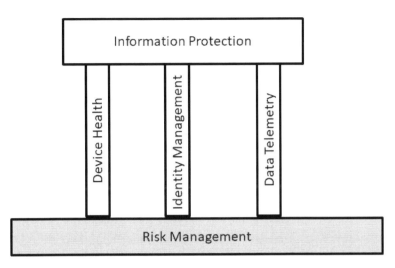

Creating a good security or privacy design or architecture means you never ever start with selecting tools for solving your problem! Selecting tools should be the last phase of your security or privacy design phase. You select tools when it is clear that the tool will support in solving your security or privacy problem. Tools alone are never enough to solve security or privacy problems. You need to fit in tools within your security and privacy processes. Several problems exist with many IT security tools that will hit you when you start too soon with the solutions instead of a thorough problem diagnosis and solution design. Wrongly selected security and privacy tools give the following issues:

- High costs;

- Complex challenges to implement and manage;

- Daily administration of a chosen tool set requires significant IT effort while it remains unclear if the tools are effective in reducing security risk;

- Overlap in functionality of security application landscape. More is not always better. To be able to justify the application of security tools for your problem a context specific security architecture should give input to the following questions:

  - What is protected with what?

  - What are the main threats we need protection against?

  - What is not protected by information security policies or tools?

– What is in scope or out of scope for your security architecture? E.g. business continuity management, safety management, financial risk management, daily IT operations, physical (building) security etc. In the end everything has a relation with information security, but you cannot cover all business aspects using an information security architecture document. The key is to focus and keep the scope clear or else complexity will become overwhelming.

– What architecture or design decisions have been made and must be validated explicitly?

– What is the model of your protection? It is far more easy to evaluate and improve a model, than adding new or improved security products continuously. Make sure that within operational security management processes learning and improving are key periodic targets.

– Does the security model cover all crucial security and privacy principles and requirements?

– Are the residual risks when this solution acceptable for the key stakeholders?

IT security in general is seen as a complex problem field, due to the many technical and nontechnical aspects involved. Since 100% information security is impossible, being able to qualify risks is crucial in getting an accepted level of security protection. Good modelling helps you to qualify security and privacy risks.

In general, it is far more easy to reuse proven concepts and models when creating your own security model. This way you build on the work of others and using a good model reference will reduce the risk of making crucial mistakes.

This section covers some commonly used models and elements that can be reused when creating a solution for a specific information security problem.

Elements that are presented are attack vectors, some examples of security personas and some great security models that can assist you when creating your security design.

4.0.2 Common attack vectors

Good security is goal oriented. Good security architecture is tailored to your situation. When defining a product or new (IT) service one of the key activities is to define your specific security requirements. Defining requirements is known to be hard, time consuming and complex. Especially when you have iterative development cycles and you do not have a clear defined view of your final product or service that is to be created.

Defining attack vectors within your security requirements documentation is proven to be helpful from the start. Attack vectors will give more focus on expected threats so you can start developing security measures that really matter in your situation from the start.

Attack vectors are routes or methods used to get into information systems. Attacks are the techniques that attackers use to exploit the vulnerabilities in applications. Many attack vectors take advantage of the human element in the system or one of the maintenance activities defined for the system, because that's often defined as the weakest link.

Within the IT cyber security world many terms and definitions are used. Attack vectors usually require detailed knowledge to judge whether the vector is relevant in a specific situation.

Some attack vectors apply to critical infrastructure components, like NTP or DNS. E.g. in a rogue master attack, an attacker causes other nodes in the network to believe it is a legitimate master. Contrary to spoofing attacks in the Rogue Master attack the attacker does not fake its identity, but rather manipulates the master election process using malicious control packets.

The good news is: The number of possible attack vectors is limited. The bad news is: The ways an attack vector can be exploited is endless. Unless decent security measures are taken to minimize attacks using this specific attack vector. Good designed security solutions are not that complicated and complex after all.

Common attack vectors are:

- Analysis of vulnerabilities in compiled software without source code
- Anti-forensic techniques
- Automated probes and scans
- Automated widespread attacks

- Client validation in AJAX routines

- Cross-site scripting in AJAX

- Cryptographic Performance Attacks

- Cyber-threats & bullying (not illegal in all jurisdictions)

- DoS Attacks

- Email propagation of malicious code

- Executable code attacks (against browsers)

- Exploiting Vulnerabilities

- GUI intrusion tools

- HTTPS Interception

- Industrial espionage

- Internet social engineering attacks

- Malicious AJAX code execution

- Network sniffers

- Packet Manipulation

- Packet spoofing

- Parameter manipulation with SOAP

- Replay Attack

- RIA thick client binary vector

- Rogue Master Attack

- RSS Atom Injection

- Session-hijacking

- Side-channel attack

- Sophisticated botnet command and control attacks

- Spoofing

- Stealth and other advanced scanning techniques

- Targeting of specific users

- Web service routing issues

- Wide-scale trojan distribution

- Wide-scale use of worms

- Widespread attacks on DNS infrastructure

- Widespread attacks using NNTP to distribute attack

- Widespread, distributed denial-of-service attacks

- Windows-based remote access trojans (Back Orifice)

- WSDL scanning and enumeration

- XML Poisoning

- XPATH injection in SOAP message

It is recommended that you specify in your solution architecture the attack vectors that apply to your use case. Remember to put the explanation of the attack vectors used in an appendix, since not all your stakeholders will know what e.g. 'Spoofing' is.

4.0.3 HTTPS Interception

In a basic HTTPS connection, a browser establishes a TLS connection directly to an origin server to send requests and downloads HTML content. But many connections on the Internet are not directly from a browser to the server serving the website, but instead traverse through some type of proxy or middlebox (a "monster-in-the-middle" or MITM). There are many reasons for this behavior, so also malicious. Most company networks and offered Wifi networks use HTTPS Interception. If you care about your privacy you should never ever use a hotel network.

Malicious forward proxies, however, might insert advertisements into web pages or exfiltrate private user information. This is both a security and privacy risk.

TLS-terminating forward proxies could even trust root certificates considered insecure, like Symantec's CA. If poorly implemented, any TLS-terminating forward proxy can become a widespread attack vector, leaking private information or allowing for response spoofing.

4.0.4 Hosting, hardware, firmware and other invisible threats

Computer security has become much harder to manage in recent years. This is due to the fact that attackers continuously come up with new and more effective ways to attack our systems. But also the emerging trend of Cloud Computing created an extra level of complexity within the field of cyber security and privacy protection.

A commonly wide spread fad is that Cloud Hosting is more secure than on premise. The truth is that it is different. Security principles and all attack vectors still apply. The main factors that make Cloud hosting more complex to manage are:

- Less control

- Technical insight in exact physical and IT security measures are often unknown.

- Influence and control on continuous operational changes on the cloud hosting facilities are not transparent for cloud consumers.

- Trust plays a great role. You must have trust in audit and security reports created by a third party. The advice is to obtain always a right to perform a security audit yourself, but at large cloud hosting providers this is often not allowed.

Whether you use Cloud hosting of host your computer services still on your own data centre all hardware threads still apply.

Since true open source hardware is still seldom seen, currently your valuable information is vulnerable due to the following more hardware related attack vectors:

- BIOS attacks. BIOS is always written to a non-volatile storage device such as an EEPROM

- Firmware attacks

- Physical device tempering. Mostly done by rewiring CPU's, CPU boards. Famous are of course the attacks on Crypto Devices (HSM's) but since hardware tempering on normal hardware is so easy you seldom hear how easy hacking on 'standard' computer hardware devices is.

- Physical data centres. Your data is not (never) secure in a cloud you do not control or manage.

An attack vector that many people forget to consider is the boot process itself which is almost completely controlled by the BIOS.

When you are still in control of your own computer hardware, consider to overcome the malicious attacks on BIOS by one the following methods:

- Digital Authentication Method
- Rollback Prevention Method
- Physical Authentication Method

Threads related to hardware are often invisible. This does not mean they don't exist. Since computer hardware is seldom open, many threads are still not widely known. In order to protect your core information you should always take measures to be able to reduce the likelihood of getting targeted by attack vectors that are hardware related. Many examples exist of poor designed CPU's, firmware, network devices, storage devices etc. with offers great opportunities to attackers.

4.0.5 Security Personas

Humans are the most important threat to security and privacy.

One of the tools of IT architects and UX designers is to work with so called 'Personas'. Personas are fictional characters created to represent the different user types that might use a system, website, product or service. Using personas is common practice when dealing with UX design. But when developing a security architecture for a new system, service or website security personas are also valuable to use. Security Personas force you to think different about the goals and behaviour of attackers that are going to hit your system.

Security Personas identify the user motivations, expectations and goals responsible for driving bad behaviour. Of course not all personas will behave bad on purpose. Sometimes mistakes on the use of the system or social engineering will affect the way a persona can compromise your system.

Benefits of Personas

Personas help to focus and help to make design decisions concerning IT components by adding a layer of real-world consideration to the conversation. They also offer a quick and inexpensive way to test and prioritize those features throughout the development process. In addition, they can help:

- Stakeholders and management to discuss architecture building blocks to protect your system.

- Information architects develop informed secure wire-frames knowing possible interface behaviour.

- System security engineers/developers to decide which approaches to take based on user behaviours.

- Testing

For security personas it is good to outline:

- Demographics such as age, education, ethnicity, and family status.

- The goals and tasks they are trying to complete using the system (or website),

- Their physical, social, and technological environment.

- Responsibilities: As implemented in future Identity and access management system, but also the formal organization responsibilities belong to the role within the organization.

Defining security personas is not hard. Some examples of security personas:

- Employee

- Visitor (in person)

- Internet visitor (web)

- Administrator

- Manager

- Director/CEO

- Angry customer

- Competitor/rival

- Neighbours

Use security personas in your security architecture so the proposed security measures can be designed more in depth and evaluated since the security personas are part of your security model. The list given in this section can be used as starting point to expand the personas for your context more in depth.

4.0.6 Threat Models

This section is not about teaching you how to model you specific security or privacy solutions. By now you know that your model should be built out of attack vectors, security personas and security and privacy principles and requirements. The next chapter of this reference architecture deals with reusable principles in depth. First we present valuable models that can be reused when created a security or privacy solution architecture.

Security threat modelling, or threat modelling, is a process of assessing and documenting a system's security risks. Security threat modelling enables you to understand a system's threat profile by examining it through the eyes of your potential attackers. Your security threat modelling efforts also enable your team to justify security features within a system, or security practices for using the system, to protect your corporate assets.

Many ways exist to build a threat model but in essence a threat model is a conceptual model that:

- helps to understand a situation and

- is helpful in reducing security or privacy concerns. So helpful in solving your security problem.

A security or privacy conceptual threat model is usually built of relevant elements and their relations that matter in a security problem situation.

In general, a conceptual model is constructed based on a specific problem situation you want to solve. In our case the aim is to outline important concepts regarding security and privacy. So our collection of conceptual models is aimed at generic reuse.

Since the real-world problems of security and privacy are outlined in a large number of publications, within this section we only present conceptual models that are based on the following selection criteria:

- Generic use;

- Non-commercial;

- Open.

With open we mean that the institute or company created the model has an open process that allows everyone to improve the model. Of course open is not always really open without borders and thresholds. Even the open group is not really open for public participation, since large memberships fees form a threshold. The OWASP foundation is however one of the best examples on how open should be. That is open license on content (common creative) and no impediments and no requirements for participants who want to join the working groups.

For security and privacy many models exist. Most models are aimed for evaluating risks for auditors and other stakeholders. In the sections below a collection of (almost open) security and privacy models.

OAuth 2.0 Threat Model

Using the OAuth protocol gives you many advantages. And since this protocol is open you can save a lot of time when making use of the OAuth Threat Model when using OAuth in your use case. A detailed description of the thread model is found in RFC 6819 (http://tools.ietf.org/html/ rfc6819).

In the picture below the visual of the threat model, where the numbers are references to the section in the IETF RFC.

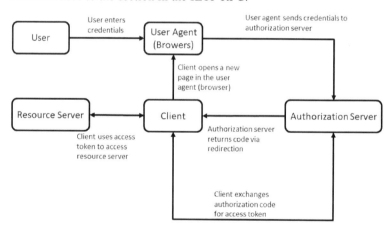

OAuth 2.0 basic model. A good threat model can be found at http:// hdknr.github.io/docs/identity/oauth_threat.html

DDoS model

DDoS attacks are hard to prevent. However, every security or privacy architecture should take DDoS attacks into account. This to design solution that are more resistant against the easy DDoS attacks.

Problems due to DDoS Attacks: - DDoS attack is an attempt to make a systems inaccessible to its legitimate users. - The bandwidth of the Internet and a LAN may be consumed unwontedly by DDoS, by which not only the intended computer, but also the entire network suffers. - Slow network performance (opening files or accessing web sites) due to DDoS attacks. - Unavailability and inability to access a particular web site due to DDoS attacks.

The model below gives a DDoS attack taxonomy. This can be useful if you are designing solutions to be more resilient against DDoS attacks.

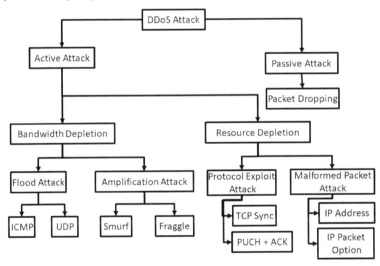

REF: http://file.scirp.org/Html/5-7800164_34631.htm

Mobile Threat model

Since mobile is everywhere, you should always take mobile threats serious in your solution architecture. Even if you think you have a special gateway for mobile traffic, most devices are always vulnerable for mobile threads.

The model presented here below can help in identifying the threads.

The diagram shows a mobile device threat model with:
- User connecting to Mobile Application
- Mobile Web Services
- Main Site Pages
- Mobile Application connecting to Local App Storage, Device Key Chain
- Device Generic OS Security
- Device Physical Security
- Mobile Device

- Spoofing: Users to the Mobile application
- Spoofing: Web Service to Mobile APP
- Tampering: Mobile Application
- Tampering: Device Data Stores
- Disclosure: Device Data Stores or Residual Data
- Disclosure: Mobile APP data to other Web Services
- Denial of Service
- Elevation of Privileges: Mobile APP has access to *

IoT Threat Model

We should be happy: The IoT (Internet of Things) is not everywhere present yet. When IoT is migrated from fiction to reality, security and privacy will be under enormous risks.

Internet-of-Things is a result of a technical revolution, which reflects with future computing and communications including existing and evolving internet. Over the time Internet technologies have evolved, and become Internet of Things. With the advent of this paradigm the dream to convergence everything, and everyone under a single umbrella has come true. Machine-to-machine (M2M), Radio Frequency Identification (RFID), context-aware computing, wearables, ubiquitous computing, and web-of-things all are considered to be seamlessly integrated into a global information network, which has the self configuring capabilities based on standard and inter-operable communication protocols .

Below a generic threat model for the IoT world:

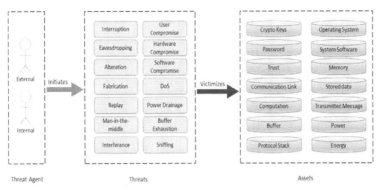

Note the view is not complete. Missing these views are:

- IDS, pentest tools, correlation tools etc (or under system security)

This IoT thread model and views are good for addressing the following areas in more detail in your security solution:

- Confidentiality
- Integrity
- Availability
- User Management
- Network Security
- Key Management
- Security Management
- Governance
- Risk
- Regulation
- Audit
- Access Control
- Standards for Interoperability

4.0.7 Security Models

NIST Security framework

Whenever you feel the need to draw a process regarding security or risk processes: resist the temptation! The US based NIST organization is a well-known governmental organization that offers great publications on all thinkable subjects regarding security.

One of the simplest, yet most frequently model is displayed here below.

IDENTIFY	PROTECT	DETECT	RESPOND	RECOVER
• Asset Management • Business Environment • Governance • Risk Assessment • Risk Management Strategy	• Awareness Control • Awareness and Training • Data Security • Info protection and procedures • Maintenance • Protective Technology	• Anomalies and Events • Security Continuous Monitoring • Detection Process • Communictions	• Response Planning • Communications • Analysis • Mitigation • Improvements	• Recovery Planning • Improvements • Communication

On the NIST site (see references) you can find in-depth information regarding all sub functions of this security framework. The experience is, is that it is far better to check what in your use case needs special attention. If you ever feel the need to create your own security framework, think again. In essence all come down to the high level framework described by the NIST organization. Using a broad used security framework has a number of advantages:

- Easier communication with stakeholders;

- Easier knowledge and experience transfer between security experts of different organization;

- Saves time, time you can use to solve the real context specific issues regarding practice use and implementation of the security functions.

NIST Cloud Computing Security model

Sooner or later you will be creating a solution or privacy architecture where cloud hosting plays a significant part. The NIST cloud computing security reference model is a very good model to use as reference.

NIST Cloud Computing Security Reference Architecture

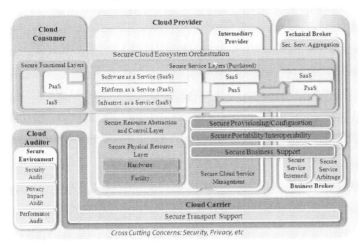

Jericho Security Model

The Jericho(tm) Security architecture model is built upon principles. The advantages of using the Jericho model for security are:

- A security architecture model built upon the Jericho conceptual model is built around maintaining flexibility and protects the most important security objects for the stakeholders.

- Integration: Easier to build secure processes with other companies and trusted partners.

- Simplifies use of public networks and cloud solutions

- Aimed for use of open principles and open solution building blocks.

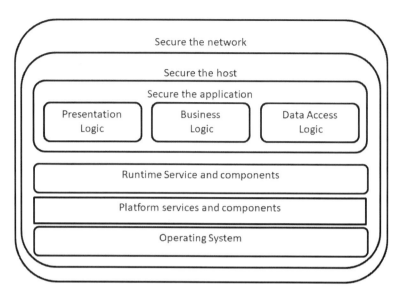

Unfortunate the Jericho framework is not a real open security framework. It is copyrighted by the open group (see references chapter for more information on this model). There are trademarks involved and all publications are copyrighted. However due to the work of many we can make use of the developed knowledge within the Jericho working group. The Jericho Forum®, a forum of The Open Group, was formed in January 2004 and is no longer active. However, the approach of this forum towards security is still alive.

Security Architecture Landscape (OSA)

Thanks to the Open Security Architecture (OSA) group there is a real open security landscape (http://www.opensecurityarchitecture.org/). All OSA material is CC by sa licensed, which means you can freely use and improve it.

Below is the OSA Security architecture landscape:

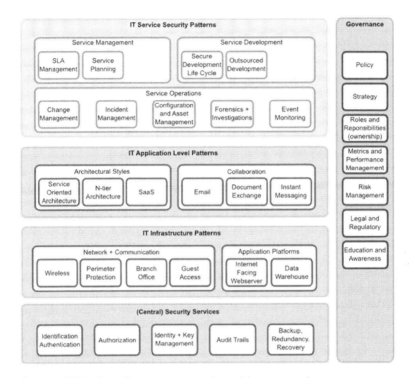

Source: OSA (http://www.opensecurityarchitecture.org)

The OSA Security architecture is based on patterns. Which mean for every pattern defined the aim of the community was/is to develop a standardized solution description. Unfortunate the OSA community is not very active anymore, so all IT security patterns around cloud are not yet incorporated.

For a number of reasons we have chosen not to use patterns in this security and privacy reference architecture. However in some cases using patterns can give an advantage. (See the Introduction, section 'What about security patterns?' for more information).

Software Assurance Maturity Model (SAMM)

The Software Assurance Maturity Model (SAMM) is an open framework to help organizations formulate and implement a strategy for software security that is tailored to the specific risks facing the organization. SAMM is useful resource if you are working on a process architecture that is needed to control all kind of aspects of software security. Our advice is to take the processes as defined in SAMM as point of departure within your security process design documentation. Formulating processes yourself in not productive, so use this valuable source of information instead of reinventing the wheel.

To get the baseline situation of your security process architecture fast in scope, you can use a SAMM self-assessment test (see APPENDIX). Using a self-assessment test you can get a very quick overview on the status of the IT security processes within your organization. SAMM is an OWASP project.

SAMM will aid in:

- Evaluating an organization's existing software security practices

- Building a balanced software security assurance program in well-defined iterations

- Demonstrating concrete improvements to a security assurance program

- Defining and measuring security-related activities throughout an organization

As an open project, SAMM content shall always remain vendor-neutral and freely available for all to use.

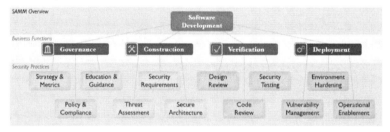

Source: OWASP

Reuse of the SAMM process and usage should be encouraged. This OWASP project is like all OWASP projects a real open project. All content is available under a Creative Commons License (by-sa). If you want to improve this SAMM framework, OWASP is a real open foundation where everyone can participate without borders. Also all communication and collaboration is truly open.

The SAMM model was first aimed at evaluating the status of software security within an organization. However due to the use in practice the framework can also be used to improve many other aspects surrounding security and privacy.

Security within the SDLC process

The view below (source OWASP) is a model of how security fits into the SDLC (Software Development and Lifecycle) process. Within almost every solution architecture you should take the SDLC into account to position where your solution fits and how maintenance is positioned within the SDLC phases.

Security in the SDLC Process

Source:OWASP (https://www.owasp.org/index.php/CISO_AppSec_Guide:_Application_Security_Program)

Security and privacy should be embedded in the SDLC process. Always. The OWASP conceptual model of the (simplified) SDLC chain shows on high level where security activities hit the SDLC process.

Car Hacking

Modelling how things really work is the best start for good protection. So any investment or use of real world hacking modles will improve your security design.

Cars and especially autonomous cars are trending. Cars are nowadays also almost computers on wheels. In order to make sure it's safe, secure and vendors do not mess with your privacy hacking cars should not be a crime but should be encouraged. Since most advanced cars are build upon OSS software security and privacy has increased significantly.

To know how secure cars are, use:

The Car Hackers Handbook: http://opengarages.org/handbook/ This Car Hackers Handbook will help you create better threat models for vehicles. Also your knowledge on how cars work will increase per page.

Robot Hacking

Robots are more and more used on various places. E.g. robots are used in homes, in assembly lines in industry and are deployed in medical facilities. But robot security is still underestimated.

The Robot Security Framework (RSF)is a standardized methodology to perform security assessments in robotics. The model is GPLv3 licensed and can be found here: https://github.com/aliasrobotics/RSF

4.0.8 Privacy Models

When developing a privacy architecture it makes sense to investigate if audit and control functions for privacy can be combined with security services and processes that are already in place. Below some models that are designed from a privacy perspective only.

Privacy Management Reference Model(PMRM)

The Privacy Management Reference Model and Methodology (PMRM) of the OASIS group can help you with:

- Analysis the impact of new privacy use cases for your company.

- Designing operational privacy management services.

- Improving services that need to be compliant with the GDPR.

- Determining use and requirements of security services from a privacy view point.

- Gives input for developing a privacy solution architecture.

When developing a privacy architecture it makes sense to investigate if audit and control functions for privacy can be combined with security services and processes that are already in place.

This model is particularly relevant to evaluate use cases in which personal information (PI) flows across regulatory, policy, jurisdictional, and system boundaries.

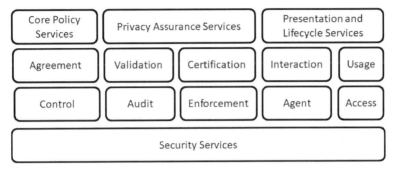

More in-depth information regarding this model can be found on the OASIS site (see references).

Privacy Management Model

A privacy management model outlines how management the various processes needed for privacy can be categorized.

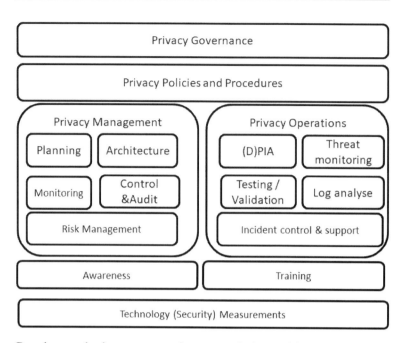

Based upon the key processes in every solution architecture a view of the various processes should be outlined. With the use of an process overview topology it is easier to map overlap between privacy, security and general IT and risks processes and departments.

SECURITY AND PRIVACY PRINCIPLES

Every organization is different. However, when you are faced with the challenge to create a new (IT) product or service having good principles requirements before you start will help. Always.

We have simplified this complex but crucial step needed in every project. In this chapter you find lists of:

- Security principles and

- Privacy principles

We encourage reuse! We also encourage you to add principles or correct these principles. In time we are aiming to create a collection of the best e.g. 100 principles for security and privacy that can be used when creating a specific solution architecture. A good reference architecture should save you time when creating a solution architecture, so use or reuse these principles from this architecture. In this way you have more time to focus on the specific context related problems. In essence the use or reuse of good security and privacy principles prevent you from making crucial design and implementation mistakes in your use case.

5.0.1 What are principles?

Principles are statements of direction that govern selections and implementations. That is, principles provide a foundation for decision making.

Principles are used within business design and successful IT projects.

Definition:

A principle is a qualitative statement of intent that should be met by the architecture.

Security architecture principles are used to translate selected alternatives into basic ideas, standards, and guidelines for simplifying and organizing the construction, operation, and evolution of systems.

It is important to draw an early differentiation between standards, requirements, and principles.

- Standards are "musts"; that is, they require compliance.

- Requirements articulate specific needs that must be met by a specific solution.

- Principles, on the other hand, are more general and serve as a framework for making choices by providing guidance about the preferred outcome of a decision in a given context.

As such, the purpose of our collected principles is to support decision making with regard to security and privacy design within all organizations.

The following criteria can be used to determine the quality of a principles:

- Understandable: Every stakeholder involved should be able to understand the meaning, purpose and implications of a principle.

- Consistent with other defined (or selected) principles.

- Aimed to the goal.

- Usable.

Principles will guide architects, consultants and designers with decision making. Within business design and architecture, you find many people with strong opinions with what a good and usable principle is or is not. Discussion is always good to get a better understanding of each other mental maps. However, discussions on what a good security principle is should be target on what you can do with principles. How will principles help you and your company? Can principles help you doing projects faster and better? Can principles prevent your company architecture and software systems becoming the next IT over complexity landscape?

Having security and privacy principles are a crucial foundation as they establish the basis for a set of rules and behaviours for any organization.

Security principles are statements of direction that govern selections and implementations. Security principles provide a foundation for decision making and are a fundament for any new design.

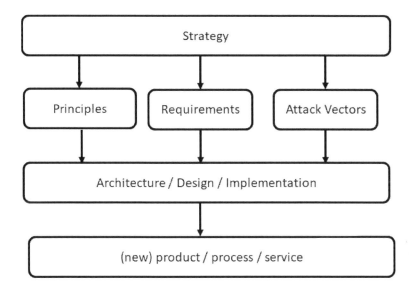

5.0.2 Principles or requirements?

The exact difference between what a principle is and what a requirement is, is a long running debate. Long running debates does not make your organization more secure. It is time consuming and in the end no one is right. So do not fall in the trap of such a semantic discussion.

Security and privacy principles have the following characteristics:

- Principles are general rules and guidelines.

- Principle are often a qualitative statement of intent that should be met by the architecture.

- Principles are guidance to help making decisions with the help of rules.

Your security and privacy design should be created based upon many design decisions. Using (approved) principles will help.

Security and privacy requirements tend to have the following characteristics:

- Can be SMART (https://en.wikipedia.org/wiki/SMART_criteria) formulated. So you can test if a requirement is implemented well.

- A requirement is more context specific than a principle. E.g. your users can have different requirements on user-friendly and secure login than users of another company.

- Requirements can be prioritized within a project, where principles are more directly shaping an architecture or design.

Principles can be regarded and treated as requirement, but due to the formulation requirements seldom can be directly used as generic principle.

Although the difference between security and privacy principles and requirements is most of the time hard to make, having requirements in addition to principles will improve a privacy or security design.

This because using requirements leaves more room to discussion and prioritization with direct stakeholders.

5.0.3 What are requirements?

Many studies show that poor requirements are a prime cause of project failure or insufficiency. Tools that assist you with creating good security requirements or let you reuse security requirements are rare. But it is crucial for good security that you start with collecting principles and requirements before coding or buying software.

Within traditional waterfall methodologies a requirements document is created by a business analysts and subject matter experts who would spend significant time on creating requirements that are never complete. Developers are often faced with challenges deadlines and have little time to handle and implement all requirements correctly. In practice there is simply have no time to get familiar with the real meaning and purpose of all requirements and developers make guesses on the real goal of requirement statements.

In most projects today, a lapse of several months would either invalidate these requirements or miss the market window altogether. Internet speed and agility mean that projects must be quick to market and must evolve continuously to meet the changing needs and demands of their users.

Common Mistakes regarding security and privacy requirements

- Basing a solution on complex or cutting edge technology and then discovering that it cannot easily be rolled into the 'real world'.

- Not prioritizing the User Requirements, for example 'must have', 'should have', 'could have' and 'would have,' known as the MoSCoW principle.

- Not enough consultation with real users and practitioners.

- Solving the 'problem' before you know what it is.

- Lacking a clear understanding and making assumptions rather than asking.

Requirements gathering is an essential part of any project and project management. Understanding fully what a project will deliver is critical to its success. This may sound like common sense, but surprisingly it's an area that is often given far too little attention.

Many projects start with the barest headline list of requirements, only to find later the customers' needs have not been properly understood.

Since security and is always in the end risk based we recommend that you prioritise your chosen requirements. We advise to use the de-facto standard: the acronym MoSCoW.

This stands for:

- M – MUST: have this.

- S – SHOULD: have this if at all possible.

- C – COULD: have this if it does not affect anything else.

- W - WON'T: have this not now, but would like this in the future.

Requirements marked as "Won't" are potentially as important as the "Must" category. Classifying something as "Won't" acknowledges that it is important, but can be left for a future release. In fact a great deal of time might be spent in trying to produce a good "Won't" list. This has three important advantages:

1. Stakeholders/Users do not have to fight to get something onto a requirements list.

2. Thinking about what will be required later, affects what is asked for now.

3. The designers seeing the future trend can produce solutions that can accommodate these requirements in a future release.

Reuse of requirements provides a number of benefits, including the following:

1. Motivation for selection of components: Requirements guide the selection of optimal components for reuse. When requirements are transferred between development efforts, the rationale behind the original component selection decision is made available to the system designer.

2. Context for reuse decisions: Requirements trace back to information gathered from domain experts and system users. Requirement-based reuse decisions are set in the context of domain processes or specific implementation needs.

3. Parametric constraints: Requirements come in many forms, including parametric constraints (i.e. the system delivered must run at speed x) as well as general guidelines (e.g. the system's interface should be user friendly) and domain tasks and processes. Parametric constraints allow a static evaluation to narrow the field of available components.

An example security requirements list:

Re-quirementID	Requirement Description	Type	Pri-or-ity
10	Sensitive data is not logged in clear text by the application.	Implementation	Must
20	Database connections, passwords, keys, or other secrets are not stored in plain text.	Business	Must
30	Encryption keys must be secured.	Business	Must
40	Privileged and super-user accounts (Administrator, root, etc.) must not be used for non-administrator activities. A secure mechanism to escalate privileges (e.g., via User Account Control or via sudo) with a standard account is acceptable to meet this requirement. Network services must run under accounts assigned the minimum necessary privileges.	Functional	Should
50	Sensitive data is not stored in persistent cookies.	Business	Wont
60	Sensitive data is transmitted with the HTML POST protocol. So GET is NOT used for sensitive data.	Implementation	Should
70	User ID must be unique. Passwords must be stored in irreversible encrypted form, and the password file cannot be viewed in unencrypted form. A password must not be displayed on the data entry/display device. Passwords must be at least eight characters long. Passwords must be composed of at least three of the following: English uppercase letters, English lowercase letters, numeric characters, and special characters. Password lifetime will not exceed 60 days Users cannot use the previous six passwords. The system will give the user a choice of alternative passwords from which to choose. Passwords must be changed by the user after initial logon.	Business	Must

For this book we started collecting security and privacy requirements, since our experience shows that all good (security) architectures and designs have similar (if not exact) the same requirements. Within the appendix of this document a link to a reusable list of security and privacy requirements on GitHub for reuse. We encourage everyone to share created requirements. See the Appendix on how you can collaborate and make the next version of this reference architecture with us.

5.0.4 Reuse requirements

Security requirements can often be reused. Many organisations have a default list of security and privacy requirements. Every project within an e.g. health care or logistic organisation meets the same context. So reuse of requirements is often possible between different projects.

You can argue if requirements for security and privacy should be stated as 'functional' requirements or as non-functional requirements. In practice since security and privacy is a complex area end-users and stakeholders have a hard time to formulate good requirements. So help your business stakeholders.

You can help by organizing a requirement session to discuss the which requirements should be incorporated into the design. And since risks are eventually business risks every requirements should be explained using consequences for business risks regarding the MoSCoW prioritization.

OWASP has a (very large) collection of common security requirements. These can be found in the OWASP Application Security Verification Standard (ASVS) Project. More information can be found here: https://www.owasp.org/index.php/Category:OWASP_Application_Security_Verification_Standard_Project

SECURITY PRINCIPLES

6.0.1 Address Privacy & Security

Statement: Address Privacy & Security

Rationale: Information is power and this is certainly true in the context of technology-enabled global development interventions. How information is collected, stored, analysed, shared, and used has serious implications for both the populations about whom data are being transmitted, and the organizations transmitting the data.

Implications: Assess and mitigate risks to the security of users and their data. Consider the context and needs for privacy of personally identifiable information when designing solutions and mitigate accordingly. Ensure equity and fairness in co-creation, and protect the best interests of the end end-users.

6.0.2 Always consider the users

Statement: Always consider the users

Rationale: The security of a software system is linked to what its users do with it. It is therefore important that all security-related mechanisms are designed in a manner that makes it easy for users to deploy, configure, use, and update the system securely. Security is not a feature that can simply be added to a software system, but rather a property emerging from how the system was built and is operated. The way each user interacts with software is dictated not only by the design and implementation decisions of its creators but also by the cognitive abilities and cultural background of its users.

Implications: Failing to address this design principle can lead to a various problems, e.g.: When designers don't "remember the user" in their software design, inadvertent disclosures by the user may take place. If it is difficult to understand the authorization model, or difficult to understand the configuration for visibility of data, then the user's data are likely to be unintentionally disclosed. Designers sometimes fail to account for the fact that authenticated and properly authorized users can also be attackers! This design error is a failure to distrust the user, resulting in authorized users having opportunities to misuse the system. When security is too hard to set up for a large population of the system's users, it will never be configured, or it will not be configured properly.

6.0.3 Asset protection and resilience

Statement: Asset protection and resilience

Rationale: Consumer data, and the assets storing or processing it, should be protected against physical tampering, loss, damage or seizure.

Implications: If this principle is not implemented, inappropriately data (e.g. user or consumer) could be compromised which may result in legal and regulatory sanction, or reputation damage.

6.0.4 Assume that external systems are insecure

Statement: Assume that external systems are insecure.

Rationale: The term information domain arises from the practice of partitioning information resources according to access control, need, and levels of protection required. Organizations implement specific measures to enforce this partitioning and to provide for the flow of authorized information between information domains. The boundary of an information domain represents the security perimeter for that domain. An external domain is one that is not under your control. In general, all external systems should be considered insecure.

Implications: Take proactive security measurements to protect secure data crossing information boundaries. Design secure information exchange interfaces (api's). Make agreements with parties involved.

6.0.5 Audit information provision to consumers

Statement: Audit information provision to consumers

Rationale: Consumers should be provided with the audit records they need to monitor access to their service and the data held within it. If this principle is not implemented, consumers will not be able to detect and respond to inappropriate or malicious use of their service or data within reasonable time-scales. In most countries this is a legal requirement from privacy point of view.

Implications: Secure audit mechanism needed. Requirements needed for audit data retention, storing, archiving.

6.0.6 Authenticate users and processes

Statement: Authenticate users and processes to ensure appropriate access control decisions both within and across domains.

Rationale: Authentication is the process where a system establishes the validity of a transmission, message, or a means of verifying the eligibility of an individual, process, or machine to carry out a desired action, thereby ensuring that security is not compromised by an untrusted source. It is essential that adequate authentication be achieved in order to implement security policies and achieve security goals.

Implications: Authentication service needed for users and application processes.

6.0.7 Authorize after you authenticate

Statement: Authorize after you authenticate.

Rationale: Authorization should be conducted as an explicit check, and as necessary even after an initial authentication has been completed. Authorization depends not only on the privileges associated with an authenticated user, but also on the context of the request. The time of the request and the location of the requesting user may both need to be taken into account.

Implications: For particularly sensitive operations, authorization may need to invoke authentication (again). Although authorization begins only after authentication has occurred, this requirement is not circular.

Authentication is not binary—users may be required to present minimal (such as a password) or more substantial (e.g. biometric or token-based) evidence of their identity, and authentication in most systems is not continuous—a user may authenticate, but walk away from the device or hand it to someone else.

6.0.8 Avoid security by obscurity

Statement: Security measurements should be open and transparent.

Rationale: Assume attackers will have source code (also for closed source software). Assume attackers will have complete design and network topologies. Open security design promote cycle of improvement faster. Assume sensitive information regarding security measurements are leaked or sold.

Implications: Do not document secrets and configuration policies (settings) in security designs. Never store secrets (e.g. passwords) on systems. Involve internal and external SME to evaluate the strength and weakness of a security design. (design review). Security should always be tested by experts (open or not). Periodically pentest the security implementation, use different companies instead of always the same.

6.0.9 Check the return value of functions

Statement: Check the return value of all non-void functions, and check the validity of all function parameters. The return value of non-void functions must be checked by each calling function, and the validity of parameters must be checked inside each function.

Rationale: This is possibly the most frequently violated principle.In the strictest interpretation, this rule means that even the return value of printf statements and file close statements must be checked. A case can be made, though, that if the response to an error would rightfully be no different than the response to success, there is no point in checking a return value. This is often the case with calls to printf and close. In cases like these, it can be acceptable to explicitly cast the function return value to (void) – thereby indicating that the programmer explicitly and not accidentally decides to ignore a return value. The rule is then only violated if the cast is missing. In more dubious cases, a comment should be present to explain why a return value is irrelevant. In most cases, though, the return value of a function should not be ignored, especially if error return values must be propagated up the function call chain. Standard libraries famously violate this rule with potentially grave consequences. See, for instance, what happens if you accidentally execute strlen(0), or strcat(s1, s2, -1) with the standard C string library. For this reason, most coding guidelines for safety critical software also forbid the use of all ansi standard headers like string.h, stdlib.h, stdio.h etc. If the function are needed, they should be written separately, and made compliant with safety critical use. The enforcement of this principle make sure that exceptions are always explicitly justified (and justifiable), with mechanical checkers flagging violations. Often, it will be easier to comply with the rule than to explain why non-compliance is acceptable.

Implications: Extra testing and programming effort:Function parameters should normal be verified for validity before being used. This rule especially applies to pointers: before dereferencing a pointer that is passed as a parameter the pointer must be checked for null. Consider automating security testing on software (static and dynamic tests)

6.0.10 Clearly delineate the physical and logical security boundaries

Statement: Clearly delineate the physical and logical security boundaries governed by associated security policies.

Rationale: Information technology exists in physical and logical locations, and boundaries exist between these locations. An understanding of what is to be protected from external factors can help ensure adequate protective measures are applied where they will be most effective. Sometimes a boundary is defined by people, information, and information technology associated with one physical location.

Implications: Create a security architecture or design.

6.0.11 Compartmentalise

Statement: Sub-systems will be partitioned logically and isolated using physical devices and/or security controls.

Rationale: In accordance with the minimise attack surface and Defence in Depth principles, this compartmentalise principle keeps a sub-system, or logically grouped set of sub-systems, relatively self-contained such that compromise of one will not imply the compromise of another.

Implications: Use defence in depth security principles in the security architecture. Sourcing of (sub)systems is easily possible when this principles is implemented correctly. Eliminate or minimize dependencies between subsystems. This can result in using other (generic) security services like a separate identification or authentication service.

6.0.12 Compile with all warnings enabled

Statement: Compile with all warnings enabled, in pedantic mode, and use one or more modern static source code analyzers. All code must be compiled, from the first day of development, with all compiler warnings enabled at the compiler's most pedantic setting. All code must compile with these setting without warnings. All code must be checked on each build with at least one, but preferably more than one, state-of-the-art static source code analyzer and should pass the analyses with zero warnings.

Rationale: There are several very effective static source code analyzers on the market today, and quite a few freeware tools as well. There is no excuse for any serious software development effort not to make use of this technology. It should be considered routine practice, especially for critical software development. The rule of zero warnings applies even in cases where the compiler or the static analyzer gives an erroneous warning: if the compiler or the static analyzer gets confused, the code causing the confusion should be rewritten so that it becomes more trivially valid. Many have been caught in the assumption that a warning was likely invalid, only to realize much later that the report was in fact valid for less obvious reasons. Static analyzers originally had a bad reputation due to the limited capabilities of early versions (e.g., the early Unix tool lint). The early tools produced mostly invalid messages, but this is not the case for the current generation of commercial tools. The best static analyzers today are fast, and they produce selective and accurate messages.

Implications: Provide awareness trainings of developers continuously.

6.0.13 Complete mediation

Statement: Complete mediation

Rationale: Access rights are completely validated every time an access occurs. Systems should rely as little as possible on access decisions retrieved from a cache. Again, file permissions tend to reflect this model: the operating system checks the user requesting access against the file's ACL. The technique is less evident when applied to email, which must pass through separately applied packet filters, virus filters, and spam detectors.

Implications: Document decisions regarding use of cached data for security services. Usability aspects should be taken into account with setting cache invalidation timers.

6.0.14 Computer security is constrained by societal factors

Statement: Computer Security is Constrained by Societal Factors.

Rationale: The ability of security to support the mission of an organization may be limited by various factors, such as social issues. For example, security and workplace privacy can conflict. Commonly, security is implemented on an IT system by identifying users and tracking their actions. However, expectations of privacy vary and can be violated by some security measures. (In some cases, privacy may be mandated by law.)

Implications: User awareness campaigns should be included in the security processes on regular basis. IT security measurements are a part of the total security system. Organization processes en policies are of great importance.

6.0.15 Computer Security Requires a Comprehensive and Integrated Approach

Statement: Computer Security Requires a Comprehensive and Integrated Approach

Rationale: Providing effective computer security requires a comprehensive approach that considers a variety of areas both within and outside of the computer security field. This comprehensive approach extends throughout the entire information life cycle. To work effectively, security controls often depend upon the proper functioning of other controls. Many such interdependencies exist. If appropriately chosen, managerial, operational,and technical controls can work together synergistically.

Implications: The effectiveness of security controls (also) depends on such factors as system management, legal issues, quality assurance, and internal and management controls. Computer security needs to work with traditional security disciplines including physical and personnel security.

6.0.16 Computer Security Responsibilities and Accountability Should Be Made Explicit

Statement: Computer Security Responsibilities and Accountability Should Be Made Explicit

Rationale: The responsibility and accountability3 of owners, providers, and users of IT systems and other parties4 concerned with the security of IT systems should be explicit.5 The assignment of responsibilities may be internal to an organization or may extend across organizational boundaries.

Implications: Depending on the size of the organization, the computer security program may be large or small, even a collateral duty of another management official. However, even small organizations can prepare a document that states organization policy and makes explicit computer security responsibilities.

6.0.17 Computer Security Should Be Cost-Effective

Statement: Computer Security Should Be Cost-Effective.

Rationale: The costs and benefits of security should be carefully examined in both monetary and nonmonetary terms to ensure that the cost of controls does not exceed expected benefits. Security should be appropriate and proportionate to the value of and degree of reliance on the IT systems and to the severity, probability, and extent of potential harm. Requirements for security vary, depending upon the particular IT system.

Implications: Calculated the cost of damage against security measurements. Take notice of legal boundaries possible and lawsuits possible (for liability) if no adequate security measurements are taken. Consider using proven generic OSS security services when applicable.

6.0.18 Computer Security should be periodically reassessed

Statement: Computer Security Should Be Periodically reassessed

Rationale: Computers and the environments in which they operate are dynamic. System technology and users, data and information in the systems, risks associated with the system, and security requirements are ever-changing. Many types of changes affect system security: technological developments (whether adopted by the system owner or available for use by others); connection to external networks; a change in the value or use of information; or the emergence of a new threat. In addition, security is never perfect when a system is implemented.

Implications: Implement security audits and pentest with your security control processes.

6.0.19 Computer Security Supports the Mission of the Organization

Statement: Computer Security Supports the Mission of the Organization.

Rationale: The purpose of computer security is to protect an organization's valuable resources, such as information, hardware, and software. Through the selection and application of appropriate safeguards, security helps the organization's mission by protecting its physical and financial resources, reputation, legal position, employees, and other tangible and intangible assets.

Implications: IT Security should like all other IT services enable to business to run their processes. So an enabling service and not a disabler service.

6.0.20 Data in transit protection

Statement: Data in transit protection

Rationale: Consumer data transiting networks should be adequately protected against tampering and eavesdropping via a combination of network protection and encryption.

Implications: If this principle is not implemented, then the integrity or confidentiality of the data may be compromised whilst in transit.

6.0.21 Data is always protected

Statement: Data is protected from unauthorized use and disclosure. In addition to the traditional aspects of data classification, this includes, but is not limited to, protection of per-decisional, sensitive, source selection-sensitive, and proprietary information.

Rationale: Open sharing of information and the release of information via relevant legislation must be balanced against the need to restrict the availability of classified, proprietary, and sensitive information. Existing laws and regulations require the safeguarding of security and the privacy of data, while permitting free and open access.

Implications: Aggregation of data, both classified and not, will create a large target requiring review and de-classification procedures to maintain appropriate control. Access to information based on a need-to-know policy will force regular reviews of the body of information. Security needs must be identified and developed at the data level, not the application level. Data security safeguards can be put in place to restrict access to "view only", or "never see". Sensitivity labeling of data for access to pre-decisional, decisional, classified, sensitive, or proprietary information must be determined. Security must be designed into data elements from the beginning; it cannot be added later. Systems, data, and technologies must be protected from unauthorized access and manipulation. Headquarters information must be safeguarded against inadvertent or unauthorized alteration, sabotage, disaster, or disclosure.

6.0.22 Declare data objects at the smallest possible level of scope

Statement: Declare data objects at the smallest possible level of scope.

Rationale: Basic principle of data-hiding. Clearly if an object is not in scope, its value cannot be referenced or corrupted. Similarly, if an erroneous value of an object has to be diagnosed, the fewer the number of statements where the value could have been assigned; the easier it is to diagnose the problem. The rule discourages the re-use of variables for multiple, incompatible purposes, which can complicate fault diagnosis.

Implications: Data should always be declared at the start of the scope in which it is used: for file scope, the declarations go at the top of the source file (never in a header file); for function scope, the declaration goes at the top of the function body; for block scope, at the start of the block. This means that declarations should not be placed at random places in the code, e.g., that the point of first use. Data objects only used in one file should be declared file static.

6.0.23 Defense in depth

Statement: Defense in depth should be a key architecture and design principle.

Rationale: Multi-layered security controls and practices are better than single defense layer.

Implications: Do not trust on security measurements from preceding functions. Prepare for the worst possible scenario. Implement multiple defence mechanism. Create a security architecture or design and document the different layers of protection. If one security service fails the security system should still be resistant against threads. Compartmentalize and work with secure boundaries for information flows.

6.0.24 Design and implement audit mechanisms

Statement: Design and implement audit mechanisms to detect unauthorized use and to support incident investigations.

Rationale: Organizations should monitor, record, and periodically review audit logs to identify unauthorized use and to ensure system resources are functioning properly. In some cases, organizations may be required to disclose information obtained through auditing mechanisms to appropriate third parties.

Implications: Audit logs must be protected against manipulation. (online/offline). All audit records should have a correct time stamp. Unified time service is needed for a secure audit service. Integrity of the audit system must be implemented.

6.0.25 Design and operate an IT system to limit damage and to be resilient in response.

Statement: Design and operate an IT system to limit damage and to be resilient in response.

Rationale: Information systems should be resistant to attack, should limit damage, and should recover rapidly when attacks do occur. The principle suggested here recognizes the need for adequate protection technologies at all levels to ensure that any potential cyber attack will be countered effectively.

Implications: Defence in depth measurement Compartmentalize IT building blocks.

6.0.26 Design for secure updates

Statement: Design for secure updates

Rationale: All updates for a system must be verified. The source of the update must be known and the integrity must be verified. It is easier to upgrade small pieces of a system than huge blobs. Doing so ensures that the security implications of the upgrade are well understood and controlled.

Implications: Verify the integrity and provenance of upgrade packages. Make use of code signing and signed manifests to ensure that the system only consumes patches and updates of trusted origin. E.g. use secure hashing (sha).

6.0.27 Design for security properties changing over time

Statement: Design for security properties changing over time

Rationale: The migration of previous users (and/or the correct coexistence of the local and remote users) would need to happen in a way that does not compromise security.

Implications: Make security design modular and flexible from the start.

6.0.28 Design reviews

Statement: All architectures and designs must be reviewed. Minimal on security aspects and potential risks. Also to determine if all (security and privacy) principles and requirements are followed.

Rationale: Integrating security into the design phase saves money and time. Conduct a risk review with security professionals and threat model the application to identify key risks and to improve product and processes under development. This helps you integrate appropriate countermeasures into the design and architecture of the application. Improving architecture and design is by far the best option (time,cost etc) for dealing with security and privacy.

Implications: Organize or make use of a structured review process to benefit from review. SME (Subject Matter Experts) must be available for doing reviews. Reserve time to improve architectures and designs or to improve code.

6.0.29 Design security to allow for regular adoption of new technology

Statement: Design security to allow for regular adoption of new technology, including a secure and logical technology upgrade process.

Rationale: As mission and business processes and the threat environment change, security requirements and technical protection methods must be updated. IT-related risks to the mission/business vary over time and undergo periodic assessment.

Implications:

6.0.30 Develop and exercise contingency or disaster recovery procedures to ensure appropriate availability

Statement: Develop and exercise contingency or disaster recovery procedures to ensure appropriate availability

Rationale: Continuity of operations plans or disaster recovery procedures address continuance of an organization's operation in the event of a disaster or prolonged service interruption that affects the organization's mission.

Implications:

6.0.31 Do not implement unnecessary security mechanisms.

Statement: Do not implement unnecessary security mechanisms.

Rationale: Every security mechanism should support a security service or set of services, and every security service should support one or more security goals. Extra measures should not be implemented if they do not support a recognized service or security goal. Such mechanisms could add unneeded complexity to the system and are potential sources of additional vulnerabilities.

Implications: Only implement security measurements when needed.

6.0.32 Don't trust infrastructure

Statement: Underlaying infrastructure cannot be assumed safe.

Rationale: Vulnerabilities are at hardware,firmwire, virtualization, middleware and application layers. To minimize data leakage risks trusting security of other objects should be prevented.

Implications: Sandbox model /Jericho model needed. Layered defense easily possible

6.0.33 Don't trust services (from others)

Statement: Services from others (departments, companies) should never (ever) be trusted.

Rationale: Security design should protect against services use of other layers or applications (also SAAS services). Systems or sub-systems outside the bounds of a receiving component must never be trusted implicitly.

Implications: Every input/output and given by external services must be validated. Authentication, authorization can be needed. Measurements to maintain availability when using services (input or output) requires strict measurements implemented.

6.0.34 Earn or give, but never assume or trust

Statement: Earn or give, but never assume or trust

Rationale: Offloading security functions from server to client exposes those functions to a much less trustworthy environment, which is one of the most common causes of security failures predicated on misplaced trust. Designs that place authorization, access control,enforcement of security policy, or embedded sensitive data in client software thinking that it won't be discovered, modified, or exposed by clever users or malicious attackers are inherently weak. Such designs will often lead to compromises.

Implications: Make sure all data received from an untrusted client are properly validated before processing. When designing your systems, be sure to consider the context where code will be executed, where data will go, and where data entering your system comes from.

6.0.35 Economy of mechanism

Statement: A simple design is easier to test and validate.

Rationale: Keep it simple to avoid risk. More is not always better. This means more components, more processes and more security measurements involved. One factor in evaluating a system's security is its complexity. If the design, implementation, or security mechanisms are highly complex, then the likelihood of security vulnerabilities increases. Simpler means less can go wrong. This well-known principle applies to any aspect of a system, but it deserves emphasis for protection mechanisms for this reason: design and implementation errors that result in unwanted access paths will not be noticed during normal use (since normal use usually does not include attempts to exercise improper access paths).

Implications: Avoid complexity.

6.0.36 Ensure proper security in the shutdown or disposal of a system

Statement: Ensure proper security in the shutdown or disposal of a system

Rationale: Although a system may be powered down, critical information still resides on the system and could be retrieved by an unauthorized user or organization. Access to critical information systems must be controlled at all times.

Implications: At the end of a system's life-cycle, system designers should develop / design procedures to dispose of an information system's assets in a proper and secure fashion. Procedures must be implemented to ensure system hard drives, volatile memory, and other media are purged to an acceptable level and do not retain residual information.

6.0.37 Ensure that developers are trained in how to develop secure software.

Statement: Ensure that developers are trained in how to develop secure software.

Rationale: It is unwise to assume that developers know how to develop secure software. Therefore, ensure that developers are adequately trained in the development of secure software before developing the system. This includes application of engineering disciplines to design, development, configuration control, and integration and testing.

Implications: Training cost (permanent) for all staff involved in maintaining the IT assets of a company.

6.0.38 Establish a sound security policy as the "foundation" for design.

Statement: Establish a sound security policy as the "foundation" for design.

Rationale: A security policy is an important document to develop while designing an information system. The security policy begins with the organization's basic commitment to information security formulated as a general policy statement. The policy is then applied to all aspects of the system design or security solution. The policy identifies security goals (e.g., confidentiality, integrity, availability, accountability, and assurance) the system should support, and these goals guide the procedures, standards and controls used in the IT security architecture design. The policy also should require definition of critical assets, the perceived threat, and security-related roles and responsibilities.

Implications: A security architecture or security design should be based on requirements that are derived from the policies defined or directly of the policies.

6.0.39 Establish secure defaults

Statement: Establish secure defaults when system goes in error or exception status, or at default startup.

Rationale: Secure defaults lower the risk of bad configurations.

Implications: Security design principles and requirements must be implemented at first release. Installation of software without safe defaults is not possible. Secure defaults must be determined and configured. Secure defaults must be regularly tested

6.0.40 External interface protection

Statement: External interface protection

Rationale: All external or less trusted interfaces of the service should be identified and have appropriate protections to defend against attacks through them. If this principle is not implemented, interfaces could be subverted by attackers in order to gain access to the service or data within it.

Implications:

6.0.41 Fail Safe Defaults

Statement: Fail Safe Defaults

Rationale: A mechanism that, in the event of failure, responds in a way that will cause no harm, or at least a minimum of harm, to other devices or danger to personnel.

Implications: Stress under load and hard failure situations must be incorporated in the security test suite. Default system configuration at start-up is secure.

6.0.42 Fail-safe default settings for security and access

Statement: Fail-safe default settings for security and access. So in case of error security should not be compromised.

Rationale: In computing systems, the save default is generally "no access" so that the system must specifically grant access to resources. Most file access permissions work this way, though Windows also provides a "deny" right. Windows access control list (ACL) settings may be inherited, and the "deny" right gives the user an easy way to revoke a right granted through inheritance. However, this also illustrates why "default deny" is easier to understand and implement, since it's harder to interpret a mixture of "permit" and "deny" rights.

Implications:

6.0.43 Formulate security measures to address multiple overlapping information domains

Statement: Formulate security measures to address multiple overlapping information domains.

Rationale: An information domain is a set of active entities (person, process, or devices) and their data objects. A single information domain may be subject to multiple security policies. A single security policy may span multiple information domains. An efficient and cost effective security capability should be able to enforce multiple security policies to protect multiple information domains without the need to separate (physically or logically) the information and respective information systems processing the data.

Implications:

6.0.44 Governance framework

Statement: A Governance framework is required for service providers of Cloud hosting.

Rationale: The service provider should have a security governance framework that coordinates and directs their overall approach to the management of the service and information within it. If this principle is not implemented, any procedural, personnel, physical and technical controls in place will not remain effective when responding to changes in the service and to threat and technology developments.

Implications:

6.0.45 HTTP header use

Statement: HTTP header information is not relied on to make security decisions.

Rationale: HTTP headers can be manipulated very easily.

Implications: Test if software does not make security decisions based on HTTP headers. Perform e.g. security tests with manipulated headers.

6.0.46 Identify and prevent common errors and vulnerabilities

Statement: Identify and prevent common errors and vulnerabilities

Rationale: Many errors reoccur with disturbing regularity - errors such as buffer overflows, race conditions, format string errors, failing to check input for validity, and programs being given excessive privileges. Learning from the past will improve future results.

Implications: Use OWASP top 10 checklist Use proven security test-tools that are regular updated.

6.0.47 Identify potential trade-offs

Statement: Identify potential trade-offs between reducing risk and increased costs and decrease in other aspects of operational effectiveness.

Rationale: To meet stated security requirements, a systems designer, architect, or security practitioner will need to identify and address all competing operational needs. It may be necessary to modify or adjust (i.e., trade-off) security goals due to other operational requirements. In modifying or adjusting security goals, an acceptance of greater risk and cost may be inevitable.

Implications: Document all relevant design decisions within a maintained security architecture or design document.

6.0.48 Identity and authentication

Statement: Identity and authentication

Rationale: Access to all service interfaces (for consumers and providers) should be constrained to authenticated and authorised individuals. If this principle is not implemented, unauthorised changes to a consumer's service, theft or modification of data, or denial of service may occur.

Implications:

6.0.49 Implement layered security (Ensure no single point of vulnerability).

Statement: Implement layered security (Ensure no single point of vulnerability).

Rationale: Security designs should consider a layered approach to address or protect against a specific threat or to reduce vulnerability. For example, the use of a packet-filtering router in conjunction with an application gateway and an intrusion detection system combine to increase the work-factor an attacker must expend to successfully attack the system.

Implications:

6.0.50 Implement least privilege

Statement: Implement least privilege.

Rationale: The concept of limiting access, or "least privilege," is simply to provide no more authorizations than necessary to perform required functions. This is perhaps most often applied in the administration of the system. Its goal is to reduce risk by limiting the number of people with access to critical system security controls; i.e., controlling who is allowed to enable or disable system security features or change the privileges of users or programs. Best practice suggests it is better to have several administrators with limited access to security resources rather than one person with "super user" permissions.

Implications:

6.0.51 Implement tailored system security measures to meet organizational security goals.

Statement: Implement tailored system security measures to meet organizational security goals.

Rationale: In general, IT security measures are tailored according to an organization's unique needs. While numerous factors, such as the overriding mission requirements, and guidance, are to be considered, the fundamental issue is the protection of the mission or business from IT security related, negative impacts.

Implications:

6.0.52 Isolate public access systems from mission critical resources

Statement: Isolate public access systems from mission critical resources (e.g., data, processes, etc.).

Rationale: While the trend toward shared infrastructure has considerable merit in many cases, it is not universally applicable. In cases where the sensitivity or criticality of the information is high, organizations may want to limit the number of systems on which that data is stored and isolate them, either physically or logically. Physical isolation may include ensuring that no physical connection exists between an organization's public access information resources and an organization's critical information. When implementing logical isolation solutions, layers of security services and mechanisms should be established between public systems and secure systems responsible for protecting mission critical resources.

Implications: Isolation measurements must be tested regularly. An audit report from a third party is required (in case of cloud sourcing).

6.0.53 Least common mechanism

Statement: Least common mechanism

Rationale: Users should not share system mechanisms except when absolutely necessary, because shared mechanisms may provide unintended communication paths or means of interference.

Implications:

6.0.54 Least privilege

Statement: Least privilege

Rationale: Every program and user should operate while invoking as few privileges as possible. This is the rationale behind Unix "sudo" and Windows User Account Control, both of which allow a user to apply administrative rights temporarily to perform a privileged task.

Implications: This principle has impact on the system, software components, but also on procedures used.

6.0.55 Limit the use of pointers

Statement: Limit the use of pointers. Use no more than N levels of dereferencing (star operators) per expression. A strict value for N=1, but in some cases using N=2 can be justified. Pointer dereference operations may not be hidden in macro definitions or inside typedef declarations. The use of function pointers should be restricted to simple cases.

Rationale: Pointers are easily misused, even by experienced programmers. They can make it hard to follow or analyze the flow of data in a program, especially by tool-based static analyzers. Function pointers, similarly, can seriously restrict the types of checks that can be performed by static analyzers and should only be used if there is a strong justification for their use, and ideally alternate means are provided to assist tool-based checkers determine flow of control and function call hierarchies. For instance, if function pointers are used, it can become impossible for a tool to prove absence of recursion, so alternate guarantees would have to be provided to make up for this loss in analytical capabilities.

Implications: It should be possible for a static analyzer to determine in all cases which function is being called, if the call is made through a function pointer. It may be acceptable to allow cases where the number of possible functions that may be called is larger than one, provided it does not affect the precision of the code analysis itself. This means that it can depend on the capabilities of a specific static analyzer what liberties can be taken with the use of function pointers. Additionally, though, it is wise to keep function pointer use to a minimum, and to restrict to simple cases, to make sure that also humans can determine accurately and with modest effort which functions may be evoked.

6.0.56 Limit the use of the preprocessor to file inclusion and simple macros

Statement: Limit the use of the preprocessor to file inclusion and simple macros. The use of the preprocessor must be limited to the inclusion of header files and simple macro definitions. Token pasting, variable argument lists (ellipses), and recursive macro calls are not permitted. All macros must expand into complete syntactic units. The use of conditional compilation directives should be restricted to the prevention of duplicate file inclusion in header files.

Rationale: The C preprocessor is a powerful obfuscation tool that can destroy code clarity and befuddle many text based checkers. The effect of constructs in unrestricted preprocessor code can be extremely hard to decipher, even with a formal language definition in hand. In a new implementation of the C preprocessor, developers often have to resort to using earlier implementations as the referee for interpreting complex defining language in the C standard. The rationale for the caution against conditional compilation is equally important. Note that with just ten conditional compilation directives, there could be up to 2^{10} (i.e., 1024) possible versions of the code, each of which would have to be tested – causing a significant increase in the required test effort.

Implications: Macros should only appear in header files, never in the source code itself. The #undef directive should not be used. Macros should never hide declarations, and they should not hide pointer dereference operations from the code. Macros should also never be used to redefine the language. The restriction of macro definitions to the definition of complete syntactic units means that all macro bodies must be enclosed in either round or curly braces. Compiler directives There should not be more #ifdef directives in a code base than there are headerfiles. Each use of compilation directives (other than the duplicate file inclusion prevention use) should be flagged by a tool-based checker and justified with a comment in the code.

6.0.57 Logging secrets

Statement: Private data (for example, passwords) is not logged.

Rationale: Protecting secure logs is expensive.

Implications: A clear message level must be built in to notify exactly what the cause of error is. Reduced risk profile on system logs.

6.0.58 Minimize secrets

Statement: Minimize secrets

Rationale: Secrets should be few and changeable, but they should also maximize entropy, and thus increase the attacker's work factor. The simple principle is also true by itself, since each secret increases a system's administrative burden.

Implications:

6.0.59 Minimize the system elements to be trusted.

Statement: Minimize the system elements to be trusted.

Rationale: Security measures include people, operations, and technology. Where technology is used, hardware, firmware, and software should be designed and implemented so that a minimum number of system elements need to be trusted in order to maintain protection.

Implications:

6.0.60 Open design

Statement: Open design. The security of physical products, machines and systems should not depend on secrecy of the design and implementation.

Rationale: Baran (1964) argued persuasively in an unclassified RAND report that secure systems, including cryptographic systems, should have unclassified designs. This reflects recommendations by Kerckhoffs (1883) as well as Shannon's maxim: "The enemy knows the system" (Shannon, 1948). Even the NSA, which resisted open crypto designs for decades, now uses the Advanced Encryption Standard to encrypt classified information.

Implications:

6.0.61 Operational security

Statement: Operational security

Rationale: The service provider should have processes and procedures in place to ensure the operational security of the service. processes and procedures in place to ensure the operational security of the service. If this principle is not implemented, the service can't be operated and managed securely in order to impede, detect or prevent attacks against it.

Implications:

6.0.62 Personnel security

Statement: Personnel security

Rationale: Service provider staff should be subject to personnel security screening and security education for their role. If this principle is not implemented, the likelihood of accidental or malicious compromise of consumer data by service provider personnel is increased.

Implications:

6.0.63 Protect information while being processed, in transit, and in storage.

Statement: Protect information while being processed, in transit, and in storage.

Rationale: The risk of unauthorized modification or destruction of data, disclosure of information, and denial of access to data while in transit should be considered along with the risks associated with data that is in storage or being processed. Therefore, system engineers, architects, and IT specialists should implement security measures to preserve, as needed, the integrity, confidentiality, and availability of data, including application software, while the information is being processed, in transit, and in storage.

Implications:

6.0.64 Provide assurance that the system is, and continues to be, resilient in the face of expected threats.

Statement: Provide assurance that the system is, and continues to be, resilient in the face of expected threats.

Rationale: Assurance is the grounds for confidence that a system meets its security expectations. These expectations can typically be summarized as providing sufficient resistance to both direct penetration and attempts to circumvent security controls. Good understanding of the threat environment, evaluation of requirement sets, hardware and software engineering disciplines, and product and system evaluations are primary measures used to achieve assurance. Additionally, the documentation of the specific and evolving threats is important in making timely adjustments in applied security and strategically supporting incremental security enhancements.

Implications: Security testing must be planned and performed on regular basis.

6.0.65 Psychological acceptability

Statement: Psychological acceptability

Rationale: This principle essentially requires the policy interface to reflect the user's mental model of protection, and notes that users won't specify protections correctly if the specification style doesn't make sense to them.

Implications:

6.0.66 Reduce risk to an acceptable level.

Statement: Reduce risk to an acceptable level.

Rationale: Risk is defined as the combination of (1) the likelihood that a particular threat source will exercise (intentionally exploit or unintentionally trigger) a particular information system vulnerability and (2) the resulting adverse impact on organizational operations, organizational assets, or individuals should this occur.

Implications:

6.0.67 Risk Based Approach to Security

Statement: Ensure that risks to confidentiality, integrity, and availability of information and technology systems are treated in a consistent and effective manner.

Rationale: Risk is the chance of something happening that will have an impact on company objectives and risk assessment is the overall process of risk identification, analysis, evaluation, and mitigation. Taking a risk based approach allows for the: better identification of threats to our projects and initiatives, more effective allocation and use of resources to manage those risks, and improved stakeholder confidence and trust as we better manage information and business risk.

Implications: The level and cost of information security controls to manage confidentiality, integrity, and availability risk must be appropriate and proportionate to the value of the information assets and the potential severity, probability, and extent of harm. Risks must identified so we are aware of what risks can occur, what existing controls are in place, the consequence and likelihood of the risk occurring, and a determination is made about how to treat those risks. Options for addressing information risk should be reviewed so that informed and documented decisions are made about the treatment of risk. Risk treatment involves choosing one or more options, which typically include: Accepting risk (by an appropriate team member signing off that he/she has accepted the risk and no further action is required) Avoiding risk (by an appropriate team member deciding not to pursue a particular initiative) Transferring risk (by an appropriate team member to an external entity such as insurance) Mitigating risk (by an appropriate team member by applying appropriate information security measures, e.g., access controls, network monitoring and incident management)

6.0.68 Secure use of the service by the consumer

Statement: Secure use of the service by the consumer

Rationale: Consumers have certain responsibilities when using a cloud service in order for this use to remain secure, and for their data to be adequately protected. If this principle is not implemented, the security of cloud services and the data held within them can be undermined by poor use of the service by consumers.

Implications:

6.0.69 Security by Design

Statement: Controls for the protection of confidentiality, integrity, and availability should be designed into all aspects of solutions from initiation, not as an afterthought. Security should also be designed into the business processes within which an IT system will be used.

Rationale: The implementation of protections for confidentiality, availability and integrity within information and systems at the end of a project is more expensive than including the security protections within the initial design of the project. Controls implemented at the end of a project are often less efficient and less integrated than those integrated within the core of the project.

Implications: Security is designed in as an integrated part of the system architecture, not added as an afterthought. Security mechanisms must span all tiers of the architecture, and must be scalable. All solutions, custom or commercial, must be tested for security. Possible areas of control which could be addressed and integrated include (but are not limited to): asset management and information classification- physical security- segregation of duties, protections against malicious code- backup- exchange of information- logging and monitoring- user access management- technical vulnerability management- compliance with legal requirements- and, information systems audit considerations.

6.0.70 Sensitive Data

Statement: Secrets are not stored in code.

Rationale: Storing secrets involves risk at all times.

Implications: Software code must be scanned on secrets (e.g. configuration details, passwords)

6.0.71 Sensitive data must be identified

Statement: Sensitive data must be identified and it should be defined how the data is handled.

Rationale: Data sets do not exist only at rest, but in transit between components within a single system and between organizations. As data sets transit between systems, they may cross multiple trust boundaries. Identifying these boundaries and rectifying them with data protection policies is an essential design activity. Trust is just as tricky as data sensitivity, and the notion of trust enclaves is likely to dominate security conversations in the next decade.

Implications: Policy requirements and data sensitivity can change over time as the business climate evolves, as regulatory regimes change, as systems become increasingly interconnected, and as new data sources are incorporated into a system. Regularly revisiting and revising data protection policies and their design implications is essential.

6.0.72 Separation between consumers

Statement: Separation between consumers

Rationale: Separation should exist between different consumers of the service to prevent one malicious or compromised consumer from affecting the service or data of another.If this principle is not implemented, service providers can not prevent a consumer of the service affecting the confidentiality or integrity of another consumer's data or service.

Implications: Sharing services between customers by Cloud Service Providers (CSP's) requires strict separation within the security model.

6.0.73 Separation of privilege

Statement: Separation of privilege

Rationale: A protection mechanism is more flexible if it requires two separate keys to unlock it, allowing for two-person control and similar techniques to prevent unilateral action by a subverted individual. The classic examples include dual keys for safety deposit boxes and the two-person control applied to nuclear weapons and Top Secret crypto materials. A protection mechanism is more flexible if it requires two separate keys to unlock it, allowing for two-person control and similar techniques to prevent unilateral action by a subverted individual. The classic examples include dual keys for safety deposit boxes and the two-person control applied to nuclear weapons and Top Secret crypto materials. Separation of privilege gives better data protection for internal fraud or internal hacks.

Implications: Security procedures are needed. Business Continuity and Disaster Recovery involve more effort. Reaction time in case of an incident can be reduced.

6.0.74 Session lifetime

Statement: Session lifetime is limited. Also for cookies.

Rationale: Security System performance

Implications: All transactions must be completed within max session time.

6.0.75 Strive for operational ease of use.

Statement: Strive for operational ease of use.

Rationale: The more difficult it is to maintain and operate a security control, the less effective that control is likely to be. Therefore, security controls should be designed to be consistent with the concept of operations and with ease-of-use as an important consideration.

Implications:

6.0.76 Strive for simplicity

Statement: Strive for simplicity

Rationale: The more complex the mechanism, the more likely it may possess exploitable flaws. Simple mechanisms tend to have fewer exploitable flaws and require less maintenance. Further, because configuration management issues are simplified, updating or replacing a simple mechanism becomes a less intensive process.

Implications:

6.0.77 Supply chain security

Statement: Supply chain security

Rationale: The service provider should ensure that its supply chain satisfactorily supports all of the security principles that the service claims to implement. If this principle is not implemented, it is possible that supply chain compromise can undermine the security of the service and affect the implementation of other security principles.

Implications:

6.0.78 Systems Owners Have Security Responsibilities Outside Their Own Organizations

Statement: Systems Owners Have Security Responsibilities Outside Their Own Organizations

Rationale: If a system has external users, its owners have a responsibility to share appropriate knowledge about the existence and general extent of security measures so that other users can be confident that the system is adequately secure. This does not imply that all systems must meet any minimum level of security, but does imply that system owners should inform their clients or users about the nature of the security.

Implications: Managers "should act in a timely, coordinated manner to prevent and to respond to breaches of security" to help prevent damage to others.2 However, taking such action should not jeopardize the security of systems.

6.0.79 Treat security as an integral part of the overall system design.

Statement: Treat security as an integral part of the overall system design.

Rationale: Security must be considered in information system design. Experience has shown it to be both difficult and costly to implement security measures properly and successfully after a system has been developed, so it should be integrated fully into the system life-cycle process. This includes establishing security policies, understanding the resulting security requirements, participating in the evaluation of security products, and finally in the engineering, design, implementation, and disposal of the system.

Implications:

6.0.80 Use an authentication mechanism that cannot be bypassed

Statement: Use a authentication mechanism that cannot be bypassed or tampered with.

Rationale: The ability to bypass an authentication mechanism can result in an unauthorized entity having access to a system or service that it shouldn't.

Implications: It's preferable to have a single method, component, or system responsible for authenticating users. Such a single mechanism can serve as a logical "choke point" that cannot be bypassed. Much as in code reuse, once a single mechanism has been determined to be correct, it makes sense to leverage it for all authentication.

6.0.81 Use only Secure Protocols

Statement: Only inherently secure protocols should be used. The protocol should not encapsulate another insecure protocol (IPSec / VPN etc.) The protocol should be capable of authenticating itself

Rationale: Insecure protocols introduce security risks than can be easily avoided.

Implications: Insecure Protocols (http for example) Only used where interaction with non-trusted environment essential. Protocol must be validated against application

6.0.82 Use standard solutions

Statement: Existing security controls should be given preference over custom solutions

Rationale: Secure software is hard. The largest, most experienced and deep pocketed software developers in the world, both commercial and open source, are constantly patching security vulnerabilities in software that has been in the wild and hardened over many years. It is arguably implausible for developers of a particular system to invent and deliver a security solution that is as good as or better than an off-the-shelf solution. Add to that the need to fully and clearly document how the custom security solution works for maintainers of the software and new developers to comprehend, maintain and extend the solution and the cost of training up those resources.

Implications:

6.0.83 Use unique identities to ensure accountability

Statement: Use unique identities to ensure accountability

Rationale: An identity may represent an actual user or a process with its own identity, e.g., a program making a remote access. Unique identities are a required element in order to be able to: Maintain accountability and traceability of a user or process Assign specific rights to an individual user or process Provide for non-repudiation Enforce access control decisions Establish the identity of a peer in a secure communications path Prevent unauthorized users from masquerading as an authorized user.

Implications:

6.0.84 Where possible, base security on open standards for portability and interoperability.

Statement: Where possible, base security on open standards for portability and interoperability.

Rationale: For security capabilities to be effective security program designers should make every effort to incorporate interoperability and portability into all security measures, including hardware and software, and implementation practices. In practice an open interface in OSS software (good documented) can be a good alternative to an open standard that lacks solid reference implementations and gives room to different ways of implementing external behaviour.

Implications: No all Commercial-off-the-shelf (COTS) software is usable. OSS solutions should provide open interfaces.

PRIVACY PRINCIPLES

7.0.1 EU GDPR privacy principles

The EU General Data Protection Regulation (GDPR).

The GDPR key principles are:

- Personal data shall be processed lawfully, fairly and in a transparent manner in relation to the data subject ('lawfulness, fairness and transparency');

- Personal data shall be collected for specified, explicit and legitimate purposes and not further processed in a manner that is incompatible with those purposes; further processing for archiving purposes in the public interest, scientific or historical research purposes or statistical purposes shall, in accordance with Article 89(1), not be considered to be incompatible with the initial purposes ('purpose limitation');

- Personal data shall be adequate, relevant and limited to what is necessary in relation to the purposes for which they are processed ('data minimisation');

- Personal data shall be accurate and, where necessary, kept up to date; every reasonable step must be taken to ensure that personal data that are inaccurate, having regard to the purposes for which they are processed, are erased or rectified without delay ('accuracy');

- Personal data shall be kept in a form which permits identification of data subjects for no longer than is necessary for the purposes for which the personal data are processed;

- Personal data may be stored for longer periods insofar as the personal data will be processed solely for archiving purposes in the public interest, scientific or historical research purposes or statistical purposes in accordance with Article 89(1) subject to implementation of the appropriate technical and organisational measures required by this Regulation in order to safeguard the rights and freedoms of the data subject ('storage limitation');

- Personal data shall be processed in a manner that ensures appropriate security of the personal data, including protection against unauthorised or unlawful processing and against accidental loss, destruction or damage, using appropriate technical or organisational measures ('integrity and confidentiality').

- The controller shall be responsible for, and be able to demonstrate compliance ('accountability').

The 'controller' is the natural or legal person, public authority, agency or other body which, alone or jointly with others, determines the purposes and means of the processing of personal data.

Since visuals are easier to handle than text, a simple visual of the GDPR visuals here below:

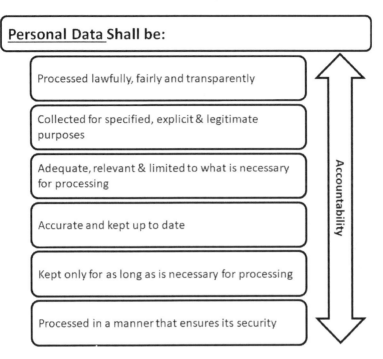

Personal Data Shall be:

- Processed lawfully, fairly and transparently
- Collected for specified, explicit & legitimate purposes
- Adequate, relevant & limited to what is necessary for processing
- Accurate and kept up to date
- Kept only for as long as is necessary for processing
- Processed in a manner that ensures its security

Accountability

Data protection should be done according by the GDPR by design and by default. However the implementation challenge is: What are appropriate technical and/or organisational measurements for protecting private data? And the good news is: If you are processing privacy related data you decide what appropriate is. The only requirement is that you must document your decisions so that you can justify your reasoning.

The risk with the GDPR is that your IT Cost will rise, due to the fact that solid quality standardized reusable open solutions are not offered by most commercial IT vendors and consultancy companies. So make use of the OSS solution building blocks that are outlined in this reference architecture.

7.0.2 Other privacy principles

Long before the EU GDPR principles was released many good privacy principles already existed. Below some important principles that are usable in many privacy architectures.

7.0.3 Access to Personal data

Statement: The organization provides individuals with access to their personal information for review or update.

Rationale: Comply with global or local regulations or legal constrains.

Implications: confirmation of individual's identity before access is given to personal information personal information presented in understandable format access provided in reasonable time frame and at a reasonable cost statement of disagreement; the reason for denial should be explained to individuals in writing

7.0.4 Data anomyzation

Statement: The use of data anomyzation is preferred when dealing with private data. **Rationale:** Easier to comply with GDPR. **Implication:** Only for business processes where data anomyzation is not possible data pseudonymization should be considered.

7.0.5 Collection Limitation Principle

Statement: There should be limits to the collection of personal data and any such data should be obtained by lawful and fair means and, where appropriate, with the knowledge or consent of the data subject. (Source:OECDprivacy.org)

7.0.6 Collection of personal data

Statement: Personal information is only collected for the purposes identified in a notice presented to the users.

Rationale: Legal regulation (local, global)

Implications: document and describe types of information collected and methods of collection collection of information by fair and lawful means, including collection from third parties inform individuals if information is developed or additional information is acquired

7.0.7 Defensive data collection

Statement: Limited data collected from users only for functionality needed.

Rationale: Only collect data what is needed for performing functionality. Limiting data collection prevents risks on data leakage.

Implications: De-identify where and when possible to reduce risk of privacy data concerns. Data must deleted when no longer necessary.

7.0.8 Design reviews

Statement: All architectures and designs must be reviewed. Minimal on security aspects and potential risks. Also to determine if all (security and privacy) principles and requirements are followed.

Rationale: Integrating security into the design phase saves money and time. Conduct a risk review with security professionals and threat model the application to identify key risks and to improve product and processes under development. This helps you integrate appropriate countermeasures into the design and architecture of the application. Improving architecture and design is by far the best option (time,cost etc) for dealing with security and privacy.

Implications: Organize or make use of a structured review process to benefit from review. SME (Subject Matter Experts) must be available for doing reviews. Reserve time to improve architectures and designs or to improve code.

7.0.9 Disclosure to third parties

Statement: Personal information is disclosed to third parties only for the identified purposes and with implicit or explicit consent of the individual.

Rationale: Communication with third parties should be made known to the individual Information should only be disclosed to third parties that have equivalent agreements to protect personal Information individuals should be aware of any new uses/purposes for the information the organization should take remedial action in response to misuse of personal information by a third party

7.0.10 Don't trust infrastructure

Statement: Underlaying infrastructure cannot be assumed safe.

Rationale: Vulnerabilities are at hardware,firmwire, virtualization, middleware and application layers. To minimize data leakage risks trusting security of other objects should be prevented.

Implications: Sandbox model /Jericho model needed. Layered defense easily possible

7.0.11 Don't trust services (from others)

Statement: Services from others (departments, companies) should never (ever) be trusted.

Rationale: Security design should protect against services use of other layers or applications (also SAAS services). Systems or sub-systems outside the bounds of a receiving component must never be trusted implicitly.

Implications: Every input/output and given by external services must be validated. Authentication, authorization can be needed. Measurements to maintain availability when using services (input or output) requires strict measurements implemented.

7.0.12 Individual Participation Principle

Statement: An individual should have the right: a) to obtain from a data controller, or otherwise, confirmation of whether or not the data controller has data relating to him; b) to have communicated to him, data relating to him i) within a reasonable time; ii) at a charge, if any, that is not excessive; iii) in a reasonable manner; and iv) in a form that is readily intelligible to him; c) to be given reasons if a request made under subparagraphs (a) and (b) is denied, and to be able to challenge such denial; and d) to challenge data relating to him and, if the challenge is successful to have the data erased, rectified, completed or amended.

7.0.13 Management Responsibility

Statement: The organization defines, documents, communicates and assigns accountability for its privacy policies and procedures.

Rationale: Management is responsible for organising processes needed to be compliant for privacy regulations and handling personal data within the company.

Implications: privacy policies define and document all ten GAPP review and approval of changes to privacy policies conducted by management risk assessment process in place to establish a risk baseline and regularly identify new or changing risks to personal data infrastructure and systems management takes into consideration impacts on personal privacy privacy awareness training

7.0.14 Monitoring and enforcement

Statement: The organization monitors compliance with its privacy policies and procedures. It also has procedures in place to address privacy-related complaints and disputes.

Rationale:

Implications: individuals should be informed on how to contact the organization with inquiries, complaints and disputes formal process in place for inquires, complaints or disputes each complaint is addressed and the resolution is documented for the individual compliance with privacy policies, procedures, commitments and legislation is reviewed, documented and reported to management

7.0.15 Purpose Specification Principle

Statement: The purposes for which personal data are collected should be specified not later than at the time of data collection and the subsequent use limited to the fulfilment of those purposes or such others as are not incompatible with those purposes and as are specified on each occasion of change of purpose. (source: http://oecdprivacy.org/)

7.0.16 Security for privacy

Statement: Personal information is protected against both physical and logical unauthorized access.

Rationale: privacy policies must address the security of personal information information security programs must include administrative, technical and physical safeguards logical access controls in place restrictions on physical access environmental safeguards personal information protected when being transmitted (e.g. mail, internet, public or other non-secure networks) security safeguards should be tested for effectiveness at least once annually

7.0.17 Security Safeguards

Statement: Personal data should be protected by reasonable security safeguards against such risks as loss or unauthorised access, destruction, use, modification or disclosure of data.

Rationale: Personal data is valuable.

Implications: Security must be in place. Security control system must be operational. (prevent,detect, react etc)

7.0.18 Use Limitation Principle

Statement: Personal data should not be disclosed, made available or otherwise used for purposes other than those specified in accordance with Paragraph 9 except: a) with the consent of the data subject; or b) by the authority of law. (source: http://oecdprivacy.org/)

EIGHT

SECURITY AND PRIVACY DESIGNS

In order to provide you with the best reusable information when creating your designs, this section outlines some key design blueprints and must do tips when creating solutions.

8.0.1 Handling privacy regulations

This section outlines simple and effective ways for handling privacy requirements within your solution architecture. An important document that is input for privacy requirements for European Citizens is the EU General Data Protection Regulation (GDPR). But other manany other countries have comparable regulations with comparable design problems.

What is the GDPR?

Privacy, security, Internet and IT systems are complex and form a toxic mix. Many things can and will go wrong. Often it is just a manner of time before real incidents happen. Since detection of privacy and security breaches is also non trivial to accomplish there is a great chance you will never known that your data is seen or copied by unauthorized persons. Privacy is a core value of individuals of democratic societies.

Tracking people without their knowledge, approval or a court order is just flat-out wrong. The fact that it can be done is no excuse. Without adtech, and massive data collection of commercial companies, the EU's GDPR (General Data Protection Regulation) would never have happened. The GDPR should put a hold to this practice. But the GDPR is no silver bullet. Many escapes are possible and without good security controls privacy can not exist.

The new EU General Data Protection Regulation (GDPR) will become fully enforceable throughout the European Union . This regulation is an important change in data privacy regulation for every company who deals with EU individuals.

Security and privacy can never be done correct afterwards. So you must design or redesign your information systems and take security and privacy as top requirements to reduce risks.

What is personal information

The European data protection law defines personal data as any information about a living individual who could be identified from that data, either on its own or when combined with other information.

So personal data is any information that relates to an identified or identifiable living individual. Different pieces of information that can lead to the identification of a particular person, also constitute as personal data.

This means that MAC addresses, IP addresses are data pieces that are defined as personal data under the GDPR. But since the GDPR is not specific on details you will not find terms like MAC address or IP address explicitly stated in the GDPR document.

Having an IP address and MAC address will not mean that you can easily identify a natural person. Most of the time information e.g. from ISPs or local network administrators is needed to determine the real individual behind an IP address.

There is also a classification called 'sensitive personal data', which means any information concerning an individual's

- Racial or ethnic origin
- Political opinions,
- Religious or philosophical beliefs,
- Trade union membership,
- Health data,
- Genetic data,
- Biometric data,

- Sex life or sexual orientation,
- Past or spent criminal convictions.

Design rules for privacy design

Design rules to do privacy by design good from the start are:

- No security = no privacy. Dead simple. You can never do privacy correct if security is hardly implemented.

- Use an open design. The security and privacy should not depend on secrecy of the design and implementation. This accounts for your core IT systems, but also for your control and management systems. So go for real open.

- Defensive data collection. Only collect data that is really needed. Limiting data collection and (long term)storage prevents risks on data leakage.

- Reduce IT complexity. Besides high cost for maintenance and change, complexity can lead to severe risks that can impact security, privacy and safety for humans.

Storing privacy data

Storing personal data or private data of others is always an issue.

The GDPR answer on how to store personal data is by using "appropriate technical and organisational safeguards". So you are screwed. IT consultants, auditors and lawyers know this and will try to convince you that the only way to answer this question is to do extensive (and expensive) risks assessments. Solid technical knowledge on how data is really stored within systems, databases, clouds, is scarce. So you will be forced to invest a lot of time doing business and organizational risks assessments and spend less time on evaluating important technical risks that come with open or closed IT technologies.

The simplest and best answer to the question is: **Do not collect and store personal data.**

On the technical solution level you will discover that you almost always need solution building blocks that will meet functionality like:

- Identity and access management

- (Secure)Data Storage

- Logging and auditing

- Encryption

You should use separate solution building blocks and make sure that when one will fail the personal data storage is still safe. So use principles like "Defense in depth" and compartmentalise among other crucial security principles.

The perfect simple secure "Data Storage" as simple technical answer for storing personal information does not exist. But smart is to standardize your IT landscape where possible by making use of reusable Solution Building Blocks (SBB's). This prevents you from reinventing the wheel for every new GDPR challenge.

Encrypting data at rest (so storing data) provides an effective protection against unauthorized or unlawful processing. It is especially effective to protect data against unauthorized access if the device storing the encrypted data is lost or stolen.

Below some tips for using (secure) solution building blocks for storing personal data, think of using:

- Make use of database encryption (All OSS databases support this perfectly, e.g. PostgreSQL, MariaDB , MongoDB)

- Make use of file system encryption or storage device encryption

- Make use of a secure Vault for the uttermost important secret information (Solid OSS implementations exist, like Hashicorp Vault)

- Make use a fancy new blockchain technology enabled storage protocol. But mind: You MUST known what you are doing, since (secure)storage of data on a blockchain does not make it private by and compliant for GDPR usage by default.

Permanent erasing of data

The GDPR introduces a right for individuals to have personal data erased. This right to erasure is also known as 'the right to be forgotten'. This means that individuals can make a request for erasure verbally or in writing. This rule is outlined in article 17 of the GDPR, but the technical consequences and complexity that comes with this rule are not trivial to implement. And a clear answer for implementation is not present in the GDPR. So even deletion is risk based.

From a technical point of view real and permanent erasing of data is a real challenge!

Using a standard delete function from a database or operating system hardly will remove data. There are great ways to get data back after administrator errors or disasters. Deleted data is often still recoverable. So simply using a 'delete' doesn't meet the GDPR compliance for erasure. Besides were do you start when deleting data? Data is often shared with suppliers, partners, resellers. But data is also transfered to various marketing companies or even sold. And data is also often stored on various on-line or off-line backups facilities. And do not forget to check if data that must be erased is present on log and audit files.

So to guarantee that data is deleted from all these different players is in practice hard to realize. Of course the key is not to share or sell gathered data in the first place, but this is not always possible. Some options are:

- If you have encrypted personal data an option for erasure is to use crypto-shredding. This is the practice of 'deleting' data by overwriting the encryption keys. However there can be consequences for data you do not want to delete if you are destroying your encryption keys.

- Use certified data erasure software. Data erasure software should comply with requirements to erase hidden areas, provide a defects log list and list bad sectors that could not be overwritten. Standards and rules for deleting data for various industries (e.g. health care and military) exist for many years already. Make reuse of this standards and rules to implementation of the GDPR easier. But erasing a data collection is often easier that only deleting a single record.

If data is or was available on the Internet, intended or unintended, is will be close to impossible to delete.

Pseudonymization or Anonymization

Determining how to handle the GDPR is not straightforward when dealing with data masking. A question relevant to comply with the GDPR is if you should use:

- Anonymization or

- Pseudonymization

To mask personal data in your IT landscape.

According to the GDPR 'pseudonymization' means the processing of personal data in such a manner that the personal data can no longer be attributed to a specific data subject without the use of additional information, provided that such additional information is kept separately and is subject to technical and organizational measures to ensure that the personal data are not attributed to an identified or identifiable natural person. So Pseudonymization is a method to **substitute identifiable data with a reversible, consistent value.** So the weakness is that personal data is still there, only a bit more difficult to get if you have no information on the used pseudonymization rules.

Pseudonymization of personal data can reduce the risks to the data subjects concerned and help controllers and processors to meet GDPR obligations. But pseudonymization of data is in general a weak process to protect data privacy. Pseudonymization substitutes only the identity of the data subject in such a way that additional information is required to re-identify the data subject. A better approach to protect private data is to use data anonymization.

Data anonymization is the process of either **encrypting or removing** personally identifiable information from data sets, so that the private personal data remain anonymous. Real anonymization is irreversibly and destroys permanent any option of identifying the data subject.

Using pseudonymization introduces a large number of risks that are not present when using anomyzation. However in some use cases you can only use pseudonymization. But use it with care, since the technical and organizational risks involved with pseudonymization are significant.

Privacy Threat Modeling

To design systems with a low risk profile for privacy and security risks a good tool is to use thread modeling.

A privacy threat model is a way of looking at privacy risks in order to identify what threats to privacy (and security) exist for your situation. Some common privacy threats are:

- Surveillance. Surveillance is the observation or monitoring of an individual's communications or activities.

- Stored Data Compromise. Systems that do not take adequate measures to secure data from unauthorized or inappropriate access expose a high risk for privacy.

- Intrusion. Intrusion consists of invasive acts that disturb or interrupt one's digital activities. E.g. network intrusion (on your digital communication) or video / audio intrusion to follow what you do.

Creating a dedicated privacy thread model is always recommended. Of course you should make use of general existing thread models (e.g. the STRIDE model) and tailor it for your specific situation. In essence creating a threat model is creating answers to the following questions:

- What do you want to protect? (E.g. What data, what kind of communication, what can be misused?)

- Who do you want to protect it from? (E.g. What people, which organizations, criminal actors etc.)

- How likely is it that you will need to protect it? (Your personal level of exposure to those threats.)

- How bad are the consequences if protection fails?

- How much trouble are you willing to go through in order to try to prevent against these threads? (E.g. cost/ money, time and convenience, loss of flexibility, etc)

Depending your domain, context and specific use case you should make use of thread models and measurements against common threads that are already invented by others. E.g. if you are a journalist, make use of thread models and tools that are already developed for you. And if you use an open model, make sure your improvements can again help others.

Fingerprinting

Fingerprinting is a solid technique for retrieving information. This can be information of systems but also persons. From a privacy and security perspective knowing how easily fingerprinting is gives input for better security and privacy measurements.

Device fingerprinting or browser fingerprinting is systematic collection of information about a remote device, for identification purposes. With the ultimate goal: To identify you as person and sell you things.

Fingerprinting techniques are so good nowadays that asking for user login name with user credentials is more error prone than identifying an user by using advanced fingerprinting techniques. Fingerprinting is stateless and transparent for the user. Any third-party interested in fingerprinting can still get some piece of information of you.

Client-side scripting languages enabled in browsers (e.g. Javascript) make it possible to collect very rich fingerprints. Browser fingerprints are also called "cookieless monsters" because it is not necessary to use cookies to collect a rich fingerprint of an user. And the good news is: Detection for users is difficult, unless you have some inside information on how a company really deals with the GDPR and how they are using this gathered personal data.

Everything you use to make a network connection is vulnerable for network fingerprinting tools. E.g. TCP/IP stack fingerprinting can be used to identify types of systems and used network configurations.

Average users are of course not aware of fingerprinting techniques used. But to give you some information on what information is (easily) retrievable when you visit a web site:

- Type of browser
- Language
- Color Depth used
- Screen Resolution
- Timezone
- Information on browser session storage
- Information if a browser has IE specific 'AddBehavior'
- CPU class of your machine
- Platform (Operating system)
- DoNotTrack settings enabled in your browser
- Full list of installed fonts (maintaining their order, which increases the entropy)
- Information on Plugins (IE included)
- Information on AdBlockers installed

- Information if the user has tampered with its languages settings in the browser

- Information if the user has tampered with its screen resolution in the browser

- Information if the user has tampered with its OS settings

- Information if the user tampered with its browser settings

- Touch screen detection and capabilities

- Pixel Ratio

- Number of logical processors available to the user browser or device

- Device memory

- Microphone, Camera (in use, present etc)

And this list is not even complete. Storing this information or pieces of this information will expose some of your privacy. Various researchers have shown that the accuracy to identify users using only finger printing technique is highly accurate. Even better than user a password or two phase authentication.

Using tools like Fingerprint2 (see OSS Privacy Applications.) within your Secure Software Development Life Cycle Processes will minimize the risks that third party service providers you use for your Internet facing systems (rich websites) are a risk for your GDPR compliance efforts. If you have a good valid reason to use fingerprinting techniques to identify your users you should ask for permission from your users if you want to meet the GDPR.

Protecting Privacy

Despite the fact that the GDPR document starts with **"The protection of natural persons in relation to the processing of personal data is a fundamental right"** it is very hard for users and service provides to protect these rights. This because making it impossible to trace communication by third parties, including governments is very difficult. Most governments are still not very kind for persons with other principles. So there is a real need to make it possible to make tracing of communication impossible without throwing giving away all the benefits of current Internet communication technologies.

Using secure communication (e.g. VPN , HTTPS) is almost a must have to be GDPR compliant. Encrypting data whilst it is being transferred from one device to another provides effective protection against interception of the communication by a third party whilst the data is in transfer.

There are some good FOSS tools available to protect your privacy if you have a hostile government and must protect your communication. E.g. take a look at Streisand, but a full list can be found in the section 'OSS Privacy Applications'

Dealing with metadata

To meet the GDPR requirements you should be aware of the risk of exposing personal information by metadata in documents. So make use of metada anonymisation.

Metadata is data that consists of information that characterizes data (e.g. Word documents, pictures, music files, etc). In essence, metadata answers who, what, when, where, why, and how about every facet of the data that is being characterized. Metadata within a file can contain a lot of privacy related data. Office documents like pdf or MSOffice automatically add author, company information and revision information(e.g. who changed what) to documents and spreadsheets. Under the GDPR you are not by default allowed to disclose this metadata information on the web.

When you distribute information or publish information on the Internet you must check if metadata in document is still present and if you are allowed to expose this information. In most cases you do not want the metadata exposed. To solve this problem a lot of tools exist that claim to strip all metadata for you from Office Documents (MSWord, PDF, etc). However in most cases these tools work far from perfect and give you a false feeling of security. For examples, images embedded inside PDF documents may not be cleaned and images also contain metadata information.

From a GDPR perspective you must be sure that no metadata is present by accident in documents you publish. So before publishing documents you should convert documents to a format that do not contain any metadata at all: E.g. plain-text document. But be aware and very careful: every format can be watermarked, so also even plain text documents! E.g. by using white space steganography. Steganography is the science of concealing messages in other messages. In this digital age with a lot of companies and governments following your communication, steganography provides still a good way for hiding messages.

GDPR tools

https://ico.org.uk/for-organisations/resources-and-support/
data-protection-self-assessment/

Specific GDRP References

The only official EC site regarding the GDPR. Note that a lot of sites pretend to be official EC sites, but are setup by commercial companies! https://ec.europa.eu/info/law/law-topic/data-protection_en

The GDPR official text: http://eur-lex.europa.eu/legal-content/EN/TXT/ HTML/?uri=CELEX:32016R0679&from=EN

8.0.2 How do I apply privacy by design

Privacy by design refers to principles that must be applied for all systems where in potential private data is captured or processed. Article 25 of the EU General Data Protection Regulation (GDPR) states that data protection by design is mandatory. However in applying this in practice can be hard. But as with all challenges within security and privacy good design rules have been developed.

A good practical guide for implementing privacy by design is created by Enisa: https://www.enisa.europa.eu/publications/ privacy-and-data-protection-by-design

A nice overview of privacy design patterns can be found at https: //privacypatterns.org/patterns/

8.0.3 How do I manage API security

For APIs that will be able to transport private or secure information a risk assessment should be completed. Be aware that APIs are part of the whole system, but for inboud or outbound APIs examing the information that will be transported by an API is a good start.

API Provider security controls are typically provided by a proxy or api-gateway. This because all traffic towards API end points is than centrally managed. You can of course also decentralize this, but than make sure all containers configurations are automatically provisioned. Minimum API controls should be:

- API key Authorisation (*)

- OAuth Authentication (*)

- Request Rate Limiting

- Logging & Realtime Analytics

- Threat Protection

- Transport Security

- Good API key security requires use of a vault.

- Established continuous code review processes

- Use of a 'soft identifier' or tag to enable tracking and analytics of the API

(* if you offer protected services)

8.0.4 How do I validate a password?

A common way to validate the password strength is to check it against dictionaries. If you want to take your password validation to the limit there are multiple list in the open domain available that you can use.

A nice collection of password lists can be found at: https://github.com/danielmiessler/SecLists/tree/master/Passwords

In this passwords directory you can find a number of password lists that can be used by multiple tools when attempting to guess credentials for a given targeted service.

8.0.5 What are good privacy design patterns?

A nice and proven way to speed up creating a privacy architecture or design challenges is to use design patterns. Good reusable solutions for applying 'Privacy-by-design' in your architecture and implementation activities can increase the speed of creating and improve the quality of your IT solution. However many documents that have a title 'Privacy-by-design' and claim to help you with this architecture challenge do little more than giving a summary of all the GDPR rules and principles that must be taken into account. So these kind of documents give you little help when you are looking a way for speeding up your 'Privacy-by-design' challenge.

Privacy patterns can be regarded as partial solutions to common privacy problems. So when you are facing privacy design challenges a good way is to find a number of good small solutions and glue these together.

A very good and rich collection of privacy design patterns can be found on: https://privacypatterns.org/patterns/ E.g. you can find here privacy design patterns for:

- Masquerade

- Use of dummies

- Data Breach Notification Pattern

- Layered Policy Design

- Strip Invisible Metadata and many more!

All these patterns are developed as mini 'design solutions' to common privacy problems. Using these privacy patterns is an easy and practical way to solve 'privacy-by-design' challenges within small and large organizations.

Adding new privacy patterns to this collection is open for all, since this 'Privacy Patterns' project is an open project. Check https://github.com/privacypatterns if you want to contribute.

This document is a reference to open security and privacy information to speed up creation of solution architectures. So the https://privacypatterns.org/patterns/ is the open resource to look for privacy patterns. This site has a nice friendly UX what minimize the time needed for finding the right privacy pattern.

8.0.6 How to handle privacy when designing new protocol specifications?

When using Internet based protocols you should use RFC 6973 (https://tools.ietf.org/html/rfc6973). This document offers guidance for developing privacy considerations for inclusion in protocol specifications. It aims to make designers,implementers, and users of Internet protocols aware of privacy-related design choices. This RFC offers always good guidelines and makes you aware of the key privacy threats that any protocol designer should know.

8.0.7 How to build the Internet yourself?

The internet has become a tracking machine. It has evolved to track you. Besides your local (business)network you are tracked by the large Internet network, corporations, and governments. Everything that can be measured is tracked. So why not build a better Internet, a non tracking network by default?

You do not need censorship or surveillance. Surveillance is the monitoring of behavior, activities. Building decentralized networks has been done and will be done more. Besides building a network to get more privacy when needed most part of the world still do not have Internet at all. So building networks to share knowlegde e.g. about privacy and censorship is always a good investment.

Check the manual at: https://bm-support.org/pdfdocs/how_to_build_the_internet.pdf

This manual is also an very good and readable document to gain more knowledge on how Internet really works.

USING OPEN SOURCE FOR SECURITY AND PRIVACY PROTECTION

9.0.1 Introduction

Security and privacy are complicated things. This is why open development is a key factor and a precondition for creating secure solutions. Security and privacy is getting more important every day. Also due to the development of machine learning applications many data driven solutions are poisoned with privacy related data.

When development happens in the open, you can directly verify if a vendor is actively pursuing security and privacy and watch how it treats issues. The ability to study the process followed, the source code developed makes that anyone can perform an independent audit. Not only on code, but also on process used!

So beside code, open development means that an open processes is followed. A process where you can see and check whether mandatory baselines and principles are used.

To increase and improve security and protect our privacy open source solutions are more and more seen as a very good solution. Within more and more companies worldwide we notice a trends towards adopting open source solutions for security and privacy protection. Governments worldwide cannot depend and trust on closed source software for their security infrastructure anymore. Gartner predicts that by 2016 99% of Global 2000 enterprises will use open source in mission-critical software. So open source solutions for controlling security and privacy are slowly but steady becoming the new de facto standard. As many security experts already known: Transparency and openness increase security protection levels. However there is still a lot of resistance against using open source for business use, especially when it comes down to security and privacy functionality.

This chapter covers facts and demystifies fads regarding open source security and privacy products. When discussing the use of open source products for security and privacy services two important question appear:

1. Why should open source be used for security and privacy functionality?

2. How can the quality of open source products for security and privacy be determined and judged?

OSS quality is a very popular field for PhD students and analyst companies. However we think that also technical experience of practical business use along with deep technical knowledge is required in order to give a good advice for a company.

Of course we have an opinion regarding using open source security and privacy products for serious business use. However opinions are to be discussed and challenged. Always. Within the technical software field sometimes we tend to see things as hard facts. For examples bad written code. Many measurements exist to measure the quality of software code. However does this means that the product is totally useless? When it comes down to software code, all software contains bugs and has more or less quality issues. If you ask an auditor to look at software code, he will write an audit report with findings and recommendations. Always. If you are hungry and go to McDonald they recommend a very tasty bad solution that works temporary. In the end with every problem you face try to find out the real interest of your trusted advisor. Is he biased? Prepossessed to get a certain result? Always try to get a real in depended security or privacy advisor when it comes down to questions that relate to your vital business risks. Always challenge the advice! When it comes down to business related questions real facts are hard. Advice is always biased. However be warned for fads! Especially within the field of open source software for regular business use. For decades many vendors have created fads regarding open source. Since this message is repeated over and over again sometimes we are weak and store these fads as facts.

Some famous fads regarding open source the use for business use:

• Open Source software is created by communist to destroy our world.

• Open Source software is made by hobbyist.

- Open Source software is made by hackers and hackers are bad. Especially when it comes down to security and privacy.

- Open Source software is never maintained.

- Open Source software is free, so it can not have any value.

- Quality of Open Source software is dramatic. Do does hackers known how to spell quality at all?

- Using Open Source makes you depended of the good will of hackers.

- Using Open Source for security or privacy protection gives unacceptable high risk, since the whole world can hack me now instantaneously.

- Using Open Source is an extra thread for my security or privacy.

Unfortunately, the list is endless long. Fighting fads is hard. Fads are most of the time a perception based on incorrect information. In this chapter we will not discuss these fads or other misunderstandings concerning OSS. However we will endorse you in this chapter with solid arguments that can help you when you are faced with fads regarding the use of open source solutions for security and privacy.

Some people are keen on ready to use list of good practices. However the context of security and privacy is very complex (organization, processes, people, technology). So we will not give a list of good practices. There are bad practices, but the list of good practices is almost unlimited, since the context for a random use case depends on various business aspects like:

- IT Knowledge and experience present in an organization.

- Information security knowledge present in an organization.

- Budget limitations.

- Time constrains.

- Maturity of IT within an organization. Especially with aspects like contracting, sourcing and IT operational management.

- Legal and regulatory aspects.

Depending on the exact needs and problems of an organization the way quality aspects for security and privacy solutions should be approached differs.

The following sections of this chapter covers the following questions:

- What is open source?

- Why should open source products be used for security and privacy solutions?

- What quality levels are needed for open source security and privacy products?

- What aspects are important when selecting security or privacy products for a solution architecture or within use in an organization?

9.0.2 What is open Source Software (OSS)?

Before even considering using open source products for security and privacy applications, it is strongly recommended that a good solid knowledge exist what open source really is.

In brief open source software is computer software for which the source code is available.

More in depth it is recommended to read the full definition of open source as provided by Open Source Initiative (http://opensource.org/osd):

1. Free Redistribution: The license shall not restrict any party from selling or giving away the software as a component of an aggregate software distribution containing programs from several different sources. The license shall not require a royalty or other fee for such sale.

2. Source Code: The program must include source code, and must allow distribution in source code as well as compiled form. Where some form of a product is not distributed with source code, there must be a well-publicized means of obtaining the source code for no more than a reasonable reproduction cost preferably, downloading via the Internet without charge. The source code must be the preferred form in which a programmer would modify the program. Deliberately obfuscated source code is not allowed. Intermediate forms such as the output of a pre-processor or translator are not allowed.

3. Derived Works: The license must allow modifications and derived works, and must allow them to be distributed under the same terms as the license of the original software.

4. Integrity of The Author's Source Code: The license may restrict source-code from being distributed in modified form only if the license allows the distribution of "patch files" with the source code for the purpose of modifying the program at build time. The license must explicitly permit distribution of software built from modified source code. The license may require derived works to carry a different name or version number from the original software.

5. No Discrimination Against Persons or Groups: The license must not discriminate against any person or group of persons.

6. No Discrimination Against Fields of Endeavour: The license must not restrict anyone from making use of the program in a specific field of endeavour. For example, it may not restrict the program from being used in a business, or from being used for genetic research.

7. Distribution of License: The rights attached to the program must apply to all to whom the program is redistributed without the need for execution of an additional license by those parties.

8. License Must Not Be Specific to a Product: The rights attached to the program must not depend on the program's being part of a particular software distribution. If the program is extracted from that distribution and used or distributed within the terms of the program's license, all parties to whom the program is redistributed should have the same rights as those that are granted in conjunction with the original software distribution.

9. License Must Not Restrict Other Software: The license must not place restrictions on other software that is distributed along with the licensed software. For example, the license must not insist that all other programs distributed on the same medium must be open-source software.

10. License Must Be Technology-Neutral: No provision of the license may be predicated on any individual technology or style of interface.

Reading this long definition can you make confused. Especially when you need a shorter definition to explain to senior management the benefits of what open source is all about.

Open source is based on three concepts:

1. A development methodology that defines a community approach to developing software, meritocracy of developers, and quality based on peer review.

2. A licensing approach that provides free access to source code, conforms to one or more "Open Source Initiative" licenses, and prioritizes the rights of users and committers.

3. A community of users and developers with open participation.

Currently open source software is software that is licensed under one of several accepted free software or open source licenses approved by the Open Source Initiative that:

- do not restrict your ability to run the software, for any purpose,

- provide one with access to the source code,

- permit one to modify the software,

- permit one to share verbatim copies of the software with others, and

- under certain conditions, allow one to share one's modifications with others.

"Open source software" is sometimes also called "Free software", "libre software", "Free/open source software (FOSS or F/OSS)", and "Free/Libre/Open Source Software (FLOSS)". The term "Free software" predates the term "open source software", but the term "Free software" has been sometimes misinterpreted as meaning "no cost", which is not the intended meaning in this context. ("Free" in "Free software" refers to freedom, not price.) So e.g. the free antivirus software AVG (http://www.avg.com) is no OSS software. In September 2015 Security firm AVG announced it will sell search and browser history data of users to advertisers in order to "make money" from its free antivirus software. Due to the fact that AVG is no OSS software, users who care about their privacy have no other choice than to look for an alternative antivirus package. If AVG was OSS software, presumable a software fork was created.

"Free software" means software that respects users' freedom and community. Roughly, it means that the users have the freedom to run, copy, distribute, study, change and improve the software. Thus, "free software" is a matter of liberty, not price.

The word "free" has many different meanings, and these different meanings often make it harder to understand OSS. The term "Free software" (as used in literature) is based on the word "freedom" (the word "libre" is used in some other languages). However, "free" can also mean "no cost", and sometimes "no cost" products come with a "catch" that in fact is the opposite of freedom. A catch everyone in the IT knows as vendor lock in or (unhealthy) dependency.

To understand the concept of free, one should think of "free" as in "free speech," not as in "free beer". Sometimes OSS is called 'libre software' to show we do not mean it is gratis. A LinuxToday posting found a simple way to express these different meanings of the word free, which I'll slightly paraphrase here:

Free can mean various things:

- Free, as in free speech.

- Free, as in free beer.

- Free, as no cost.

- Free, as high on drugs

They are not all the same.

Free software(FOSS): Richard Stallman's Free Software Definition, adopted by the Free Software Foundation (FSF), defines free software as a matter of liberty, not price.

So summarized: Open source software (OSS) has nothing to do with no cost or no value. The initial cost structure for acquiring OSS based solutions is different. A license fee for the software use is absent. However to keep your solution supported by a vendor most companies pay a regular maintained fee to keep quality ask risk as low as possible. This is equal as with closed software solutions.

9.0.3 The power of open for security and privacy

To make improve security and privacy within digital worlds a number of aspects are of crucial importance:

- Open collaboration: This means that everyone can reuse and/or improve security and privacy related material (e.g. documentation).

- Use of open solutions: This means the application of OSS products for more and more security and privacy services. Many papers and books are written of the business advantage of using OSS software. When it comes down to security the main principle to go for OSS is openness. Using open solutions makes the solutions in the end more resistant against vulnerabilities. In the end it is about transparent facts and quality criteria everyone can evaluate if needed. With closed source solution validation of quality statements is often not for all stakeholders possible. Think about the use of simple encryption software: We have more trust in an open encryption solutions that one that is claimed by a company that is unbreakable.

- Learn from each other and from our mistakes. People make mistakes. We make bad designs that increases security problems instead of solving them. OSS projects are not always managed as they should be when they produce critical security software. Learning in an open collaborative way without any direct or indirect commercial interest is crucial to get security and privacy aspects in IT where they should be: Just some quality criteria within the whole range of important aspects. In future the emphasis on security and privacy is equal as on safety, usability and business continuity. Currently only for safety aspects mandatory policies exist for companies to prevent people dying from software bugs. But today security and privacy aspects are not handled in the same way as safety aspects. A different approach is taken when it comes to designing IT systems on which human lives depend compared to designing information and privacy aspects in (business) information systems.

- Openness. Full Transparency is needed when it comes to privacy. OSS and especially OSS software that can be hosted on premise is well positioned to ensure privacy when it comes to your digital footprints. Free Software is probably the only way to ensure that.

Improvements will not come overnight and a paradigm shift is needed for many companies to be more open and transparent regarding their security and privacy designs. Since privacy data is a core asset of customers of all companies, in future customers will demand a full transparent view on how a company protects the value assets given by customers.

Open security can be defined as an approach to use existing open knowledge in combination with the application of open source software (OSS) to help solve cyber security problems. OSS approaches collaboratively

develop and maintain intellectual works (including software and documentation) by enabling us to use them for any purpose, as well as study,
create, change, and redistribute them (in whole or in part).

Cyber security problems are created by starting with bad architecture or
design or simply by a lack of knowledge and experience. Using an open
security approach the security can be improved through collaboration.

So why use open source software for security and privacy applications?
Open source software provides additional trust by allowing people to
look into the source code whereas good OSS projects are completely
transparent on all their SDLC and quality processes. When using OSS
adjustments or improvements are easily made providing you with a flexible solution for your business.

Summary: Open source for use in the field of security and privacy means
easy reuse (code or ideas), to improve what is already there. Reuse would
be in a way so everyone can benefit. That way the quality gets better and
better.

9.0.4 Determining quality of OSS for security and privacy applications

What quality really is or not has been a long running debate in many
(scientific) management books. So it is only logic that quality in open
source has been also a long running debate. However the fads regarding OSS made these discussions even harder to get a clear view on what
should be defined as quality in relation to OSS security and privacy products. If you are planning to join these discussions, we would like to warn
you to beware that these discussions are biased with many fads and un-
proven facts. Also many opinions in this field take an almost religious
turn. General statements and general discussion seldom lead to weighted
balanced judgment. IT for business use or security is not only the field of
scientific computer science. Social sciences play a great role within IT
security and privacy (think of the many awareness campaigns), and the
field of risk management is not only the field of statisticians and mathe-
maticians, but also psychology plays a role.

In essence the definition of quality and good OSS quality largely depends
on the goal and context of the specific use case.

Quality and trust are for security and privacy products one of the most
important aspects. This section will give guidelines on how quality of

open source software for security and privacy can be easily measured and judged depending on your goal and use case.

Determination of the quality of security and privacy for a specific use case is complex. Besides an approved OSS licensed (see http://opensource.org) an OSS security products requires far more quality aspects. A license alone is not enough. This section describes a checklist to assist in evaluating the quality of an OSS products targeted on security and privacy. OSS products should always be evaluated on quality before use for real. But security and privacy OSS products have the following points that make evaluating a bit different:

- Trust

- Security (Unfortunately many security products are insecure and require insecure configuration to be usable!)

- Maintenance. Due to the SSL Heartbleed bug (http://heartbleed.com/) maintenance of OSS security products has grown in importance.

- Safety aspects can be compromised if security and privacy aspects are not handled well. Recent examples are car-hacking and plane-hacking. Due to security flaws, the safety can be compromised if intruders get into a system. Also personal safety (where do people live that . . .) can be harmed if for example web shops are sloppy with personal data and order records. Criminals like list of persons who buy very expensive paintings online.

The use of Open Source Software (OSS) components is a viable alternative to Commercial Off-The-Shelf (COTS) security and privacy components. Since the quality of OSS products varies widely, both industry and the research community have reported several OSS evaluation methods that are tailored to the specific characteristics of OSS. We have performed a systematic identification and evaluation of many of these methods, and present in this section the factors that really make sense with respects to:

- The endless types of context specific organizations that potentially use OSS security and privacy products.

- Protect (very)small and large security and privacy OSS projects who have very high product quality, but score less on (visible) process quality aspects.

- The variety in which security and privacy OSS products can be used within a SDLC.

The latest and most promising project for potential users to get a fast insight in OSS security projects is the "Core Infrastructure Initiative Best Practices Badge" project of the linuxfoundation.org. Badge will hopefully give in future some indication on some quality aspects regarding OSS security products. However the badges project has a specific scope and not all value reusable OSS software and projects are able to gain a badge. But also if an OSS has a badge, it still will be important to evaluate the use and risks for your use case.

A good security and privacy product should at least be evaluated on:

- Product quality aspects;

- Process quality aspects and

- Quality control system used to preserve product and process quality

In order to cut the complexity and not write endless notes on what quality is and how it can be measured we will focus in this section on given ready-to-use evaluation criteria. Use, reuse , or improve them. We will also try to collaborate with the badges project and similar OWASP projects to get one open evaluation list in future that is easy to use.

Note that some evaluation criteria are more important than others, but since quality is always context related evaluating the many different aspects further in depth should be done in a context specific solution architecture, not in this (general) reference architecture.

To keep things organized we use:

- ISO 25010 standard for software product quality (successor of the ISO 9126 standard)

- ISO/IEC15288 System Lifecycle Processes.

Note that ISO 25010 lacks attention for aspects like:

- Functional requirements

- Compliance (e.g. with laws, standards) requirements

- Documentation, Support and Training requirements

To overcome these aspects, we use our security and privacy principles in order to get an in-depth list of criteria that can be used for evaluation.

The following evaluation model is used:

Our main goal is to present in this reference architecture a list of evaluation criteria as simple as possible. So we enriched the criteria with simple (example) questions.

In the following paragraph key questions are given that can be used to evaluate an OSS security or privacy application for your use case.

Architecture and design

OSS projects that produce security or privacy software, solutions, libraries etc. should have:

- Defined principles.

- Defined requirements.

- Make reuse of e.g. good security and privacy standards to avoid reinventing the wheel.

- Readable architecture or design. So also people who are not programmers can understand the design. At least all design decision should be documented.

Unfortunately good security or privacy architectures and designs are rare for IT projects. This does not only account to large governmental projects, but also for large OSS security projects. Mind also that a big OSS security or privacy project can mean different things:

- Large number of users of a product or
- Enormous amount of source code
- Significant number of full time maintainers (over 10 is already a huge amount)
- Enormous number of contributors to a project.
- Etc.

E.g. the OpenSSL project has many users worldwide, however since the number of active project members was dramatically small, large is no guarantee for sustainable good quality.

Maintainability

When using OSS software you must have a strategy and a process that handles the maintenance of the software. Maintenance is essential for security and privacy related software products.

Maintenance has many aspects. For a healthy OSS security and privacy application you can divide maintenance in:

1. Maintenance on the OSS software product itself;
2. Maintenance on the quality system built around the eco system (processes, organization, financial s, control procedures, contributors and maintainers stability, etc.)
3. Maintenance process required for using the product.

Since this section only covers guidelines for evaluation of quality aspects of OSS security and privacy products we will only deal with the maintenance aspects directly related to the OSS product and organization surrounding it. But please beware: The maintenance required to be organized by you or your organization can differ significantly per OSS product. Some OSS security and privacy projects are aimed at making maintenance processes needed within your organization as simple as possible where other projects require more effort. Critical evaluation questions are:

- Is there a transparent way for (new)requirements adoption?
- Is there a strict change management process?

- Is there a tough release scheme? (A release early, release often (sometimes abbreviated RERO) approach). E.g. every month a new release.

- Is there a stable release and an alfa or beta release with new features?

- Is there an active community of developers?

- Are security vulnerabilities fixed in a structured way?

- Is there a source code release and a binary code release?

- What is the frequency of updates for the OSS project?

- Does the project use a build system that can automatically rebuild the software?

- Is there an automated test suite available?

- Are new tests always added for new functionality? (E.g. due to a internal policy?)

Maintainability plays a special role for open source cryptographic software algorithms. Cryptographic software requires next to excellent programming skills deep knowledge of cryptography. To be able to maintain cryptographic software finding the right resources is very hard. Within the security principle section some principles can be found that relate to quality aspects formulated for cryptographic software.

Reliability

Whenever you use an OSS security or privacy product you rely on protection or functionality. Reliability is a core aspect when evaluating OSS security and privacy products. Critical evaluation questions for reliability are:

- Is there an automatic test suite for the product?

- Does the testing methodology include (automatic) regression tests?

- Are interfaces with other products and platforms tested?

- Is there a written test plan along with documented test results?

- Are test reports published on the website?

- Is the software tested (when relevant) against OWASP top 10 vulnerabilities?

- Is the OWASP Application Security Verification Standard (ASVS) met?

- Is there a public accessible defects database?

- Is there a process organized around defects management?

- Is there a standard procedure followed before release new software in stable versions?

- Is the quality process documented?

- Is an endurance test under stress load performed with the public released version? Is this test public so everyone can (re)use it? (note: Not for all applications relevant)

- Has the project a website with a static URL?

- Is it clear who are project members, contributors and committers?

- Does a written procedure exist on how one can get commit rights on the core repository?

- Is there a public audit log available of changes on the core repository? (Subversion, Git and many other SSCM systems provide this crucial feature.)

- Are the SANS Securing Web Application Technologies (SWAT) criteria met?

Security

When using an OSS product you trust it is secure. Security is of course about trust, but when you use OSS security and privacy tools you must evaluate some crucial security aspects.

Unfortunately many security products exist that decrease your security. Software that requires insecure configurations for example or many non-standard network sockets is not a good example of decent security.

Even if you are only testing a product or evaluating, you must have some criteria in place to prevent downloading malware or worse.

Some critical questions to determine some security aspects are:

- Are security vulnerabilities fixed according to a described process?

- Does the project have its own security officer or security team?

- Does a procedure exist and is it followed for performing a static and dynamic security code review on every major release? Are results of the secure code reviews available?

- A dynamic analysis tool for the code is used before releasing a major version (e.g. the project may use a fuzzing tool (e.g., American Fuzzy Lop) or a web application scanner (e.g., OWASP ZAP or w3af).

- What kind of socket connections and protocols have been used? Standard sockets connections (22,443,80,445) and standard protocols used (e.g. HTTPS, SSH, SSL, LDAP, LDAPs)?

- Are product vulnerabilities mentioned in the CVE database?

- Is it clear how many vulnerabilities (open and fixed) are mentioned in the CVE database? (Use the http://web.nvd.nist.gov/view/vuln/search?execution=e2s1) and search on product name. Note that vulnerabilities can be reported on the core product, but also on additional contributed modules if you are investigating a large OSS project.

- Is there a process to deal with vulnerabilities (e.g. release of fixed/patches in a controlled manner).

- Has the project created its own cryptographic libraries? Note that writing cryptographic algorithms is very hard and should be prevented by using already available good OSS algorithms.

- If cryptographic protocols or libraries are used, have these algorithms been published and reviewed by experts?

- Security and privacy principles and requirements are defined for the project and within the design and implementation it is clear how these are covered.

- All vulnerabilities are reported on the project site and are accessible without limitation by the public.

- It is clearly documented what process must be followed to obtain change rights on the main software repository.

- Procedures and policies exist to protect the code base from vandalism.

- Is a software release signed by a hash (minimal sha1 or stronger)?

Privacy

When you use an OSS security or privacy product you should not be required to register your name and organization in a database if it only serves a marketing purpose. All OSS licenses are very clear on what is allowed regarding distribution. People may sell OSS software. Even the GPL allows this. But since privacy aspects are becoming more and more important you must be aware on critical aspects that can harm your privacy when using OSS security or privacy tools.

Some critical questions to determine and evaluate privacy aspects are:

- The project has a clear written privacy policy on the website.
- Tracking cookies and other finger printing techniques are not used on the project core community website.
- The OSS security and privacy project respects the privacy of its users and contributors in all possible ways.
- Project maintainers and contributors are allowed to participate under an alias since not all governments allow working on OSS privacy or security products.
- The project is clear on measurements for handling contributors' personal identifiable data.
- Privacy of users or companies using the product is neither exposed nor stored.
- No privacy related data is stored and used by the project.

Change control

There can be no progress without change and if change is not taking place the bit rot will start. For security and privacy OSS projects some change control LCM aspects are of crucial importance. To make implementation of changes easy more and more projects enable an automatic update service that automatically implements changes on all running software instances. However implementing such a mechanism requires a very high level of internal change and governance processes.

Some questions to determine and evaluate change control aspects are:

- Has the project a version-controlled source repository that is publicly readable?

- Does the OSS project uses tools and principles to make builds reproducible? preferred is that the OSS software is build using the https://reproducible-builds.org/ standards.

- Is issue tracking for defects in place? (For reporting bugs or feature request).

- Is tracking of requirements or enhancement on requirements request in place?

- Does the project release software with unique version numbering?

- Is a change log in human readable format for each release available?

- Does a clear documented SLCM process for the project exist?

- Is it clear how automatically built CI environments are configured and maintained?

- Does the change control process allow roll backs of releases?

Whilst anyone can inspect the source code of free and open source software for malicious flaws, most software is distributed pre-compiled with no method to confirm whether they correspond. So for change control it is crucial that software builds are fully reproducible. Creating real reproducible software build is a complicated tasks. However the tools and infrastructure offered by the https://reproducible-builds.org/ makes this transparent and a bit simpler.

Documentation

Software source code is not uniquely readable. Not everyone is a programmer and there is a huge number of dialects. Software code can be for example GO, Java, C/C++,PHP, Perl, Python, Javascript, Erlang, Scale etc. To be able to use software, configure it and get a quick impression of the quality of the project documentation is crucial. A project with good and solid documentation provides trust. Large popular OSS security and privacy projects will have many (commercial) books available. Good documentation creates good projects. Bad or not maintained documentation can kill a project.

Some questions to determine and evaluate documentation aspects to investigate the quality of an OSS security and privacy application are:

- Is documentation for new developers available for free on the website?

- Is the source code documented?

- Is documentation maintained?

- Does a structured written procedure exist on how the documentation is maintained?

- Are documentation processes embedded in the CI pipeline?

- Are the user manuals provided by the project?

- Is it directly clear what the status of the documentation is? Programmers usually do not write the user documentation. But it is crucial that the documentation keeps in sync with every release.

- Are there (many) books (besides the one published by the project itself) available?

- Is commercial documentation available (e.g. books on Amazone)?

- Can everyone participate in improving the documentation?

- Is the documentation published under a Creative Commons licenses (CC) license?

Community

All solid OSS security and privacy projects have a strong and stable community. By evaluating community aspects one can get an indication on how the project deals with all kind of crucial quality aspects on product level and on process level. A community does not have to be large and very active. Many good security projects exist with 2-3 community members who manage to perform all crucial processes on a periodic basis. Stability is often more important than size. An OSS project that has too many forks can be an indication of a strong vision of the leader or a lack of leadership on dealing with crucial issues regarding the project health. A fork is most of the time a good sign. It means the software is used in many different ways and some people are building other communities to support their future vision for the project. But some research on why a project is forked should be done when you are evaluating OSS security products that offer exact the same functionality and share the same code base.

Some questions that can assist you in evaluation community related aspects:

- How big is the community of core developers?
- Is the process of joining the OSS project transparent?
- Is it clear how one can become a code submitter?
- Is the process around the core community open and transparent?
- Are commercial books of the project available?
- What is the number of available commercial books of the project?
- Are many books available? (E.g. on amazon.com or O'Reilly)
- Are mailing lists of the core developers open and transparent?
- Is it clear how decisions are made within the project?
- Can everyone attend to all project discussions (e.g. mailing list, slack channels, IRC)?
- Average number of people active on IRC or slack?
- The project has a written policy to stay active and healthy (e.g. the C4, see zmq)

Integration

Using OSS security or privacy software is always done in a specific context. You already have other software building blocks, you need your own reports, or you want to use another identity manager to use the product. Integration aspects on business and technical level are crucial for healthy OSS security and privacy projects. Too often projects fall victim to scope creep and are creating a one-size-fits-all solution. Logging, auditing and encryption e.g. are services are a world of themselves. The same goes for great responsive GUI's. You cannot create an excellent CMS when you are focusing on a dedicated security or privacy function.

Some questions that can help you evaluate integration aspects of OSS security and privacy products:

- Can the software easily be integrated with non OSS or other OSS projects?
- Does the software allow an easy way to extend its functionality?

- Is the software modular built?
- Are REST interfaces available?
- Are all interfaces for external use stateless by design?
- Are API's well documented?
- Does the OSS license have impact on building your own library or module against the core product? E.g. the GPL is very clear on integration.
- Is it clear how security or privacy aspects are impacted when third party integration modules are used?

Support

Every organization using OSS security and privacy products sooner or later needs some professional support to maintain the product, to adjust configuration settings or to implement new versions. Within many businesses support on software is crucial and it is often written down in lengthy support contracts with many sentences that must make clear what kind of support is requested. In general, when you have a good relationship with a company that supports some (OSS) software for you, the contract should be based more on trust. Lengthy contracts are usually the result of little confidence or expensive mistakes made in the past. The great advantage of using OSS security and privacy products is that you can be very flexible in how you organize crucial support issues for a product. Of course when you rebuild the product it will be hard to find people who can easily resolve problems. Some OSS security and privacy products have a commercial version for which you can get paid support. But when the commercial version differs from the OSS version you are not dealing with a healthy OSS project anymore.

A large and well known OSS security and privacy project has many excellent people within the community who are willing to provide support.

Some questions that help you evaluate support aspects regarding OSS security and privacy products:

- Is paid support possible?
- Is there a strong community support?
- Can questions on usage, configuration or problems be posted somewhere?

- Has the project an active open forum or mailing list for support questions?

- Does a mailing list exist for paid support or contracting work corporate users of the product?

- Is it possible to contact one of the core developer(s) working on the product directly (e.g. email?)

Legal

Security and privacy application can have many legal aspects. This applies not only to the usage, but also to the possession and creation of security and privacy related software. Many governments suspect people who use encryption software for private use. In some countries the use of privacy protection tools is prohibited. When using OSS security and privacy products it can be crucial to evaluate the legal aspects first, before using the product. Many security or privacy OSS products are great tools for criminals. This cannot be avoided. When someone uses a tablet to smash people on the head Apple cannot be accused of creating a murder weapon. However responsible projects are aware of possible trivial misuse.

Some questions that can help you evaluate legal aspects of OSS security and privacy products:

- Which OSS license is used?

- Is the license approved by the OSI foundation?

- Is the OSS license a widely used license?

- All functionality must meet the **Open Standards Requirement for Software** by the Open Source Initiative

- Is the OSS project aware of any possible misuse of the product? E.g. does a notice exist on what the intention for correct usage is of the product?

- Can you be held responsible for damage or lawbreaking when you use the product on the open internet? Does the project warn you for this kind of aspects?

OSS SECURITY APPLICATIONS

10.0.1 About this list

We know we can never be complete with an overview of OSS security and privacy applications. The overview in this chapter is created end of 2019-Q1 and is just a guidance to give you:

- Insights on what type of products are available in the OSS domain.

- A collection of OSS solution building blocks for your security architecture or design you can consider to evaluate for your specific use case.

- Some ideas of solutions you are perhaps not familiar with.

An up-to-date list is always online.

There are now a million different open source software projects published somewhere on the internet. Our holy grail is to keep track of the top 50 security and privacy open source projects for every security and privacy service needed within a business architecture. This way when you need a secure logging service you can evaluate the top 50 projects first before searching further or creating (aka forking) your own. In this first release of this OSS Security and Privacy reference architecture we yet are far away from this goal.

Criteria used for products mentioned in this chapter are:

- The products must have a valid OSS license;

- The project must be active and must meet a certain quality level;

- The product must be in use somewhere (*)

(*) Unfortunately we can and never will expose information where products are in use, however many mature products have solid references on their website, along with active user groups.

10.0.2 AIL framework

AIL is a modular framework to analyse potential information leaks from unstructured data sources like pastes from Pastebin or similar services or unstructured data streams. AIL framework is flexible and can be extended to support other functionalities to mine or process sensitive information (e.g. data leak prevention).

Many features are provided within this framework. E.g.:

- Modular architecture to handle streams of unstructured or structured information.

- Default support for external ZMQ feeds, such as provided by CIRCL or other providers.

- Multiple feed support: Each module can process and reprocess the information already processed by AIL.

- Detecting and extracting URLs including their geographical location (e.g. IP address location).

- Extracting and validating potential leak of credit cards numbers, credentials, . . .

- Extracting and validating email addresses leaked including DNS MX validation.

- Module for extracting Tor .onion addresses (to be further processed for analysis).

- Keep tracks of duplicates (and diffing between each duplicate found) Extracting and validating potential hostnames (e.g. to feed Passive DNS systems).

- A full-text indexer module to index unstructured information Statistics on modules and web.

SBB License	GNU Affero General Public License Version 3
Core Technology	Python
Project URL	https://github.com/CIRCL/AIL-framework
Source Location	https://github.com/CIRCL/AIL-framework
Tag(s)	Python, Security

10.0.3 American fuzzy lop

American fuzzy lop is a security-oriented fuzzer that employs a novel type of compile-time instrumentation and genetic algorithms to automatically discover clean, interesting test cases that trigger new internal states in the targeted binary. This substantially improves the functional coverage for the fuzzed code.

These tool can be very productive in determining security flaws: The famous SSL Heartbleed bug was found in record time using this software. See https://blog.hboeck.de/archives/868-How-Heartbleed-couldve-been-found.html.

SBB License	GNU General Public License (GPL) 2.0
Core Technology	C
Project URL	http://lcamtuf.coredump.cx/afl/
Source Location	http://lcamtuf.coredump.cx/afl/releases/
Tag(s)	Security, Test Tool

10.0.4 Bandit

Bandit is a tool designed to find common security issues in Python code. To do this Bandit processes each file, builds an AST from it, and runs appropriate plugins against the AST nodes. Once Bandit has finished scanning all the files it generates a report.

Bandit was originally developed within the OpenStack Security Project and later rehomed to PyCQA.

SBB License	Apache License 2.0
Core Technology	Python
Project URL	https://github.com/PyCQA/bandit
Source Location	https://github.com/PyCQA/bandit
Tag(s)	Security, Vulnerability scanning

10.0.5 Bosun

Bosun is an open-source, MIT licensed, monitoring and alerting system by Stack Exchange. It has an expressive domain specific language for evaluating alerts and creating detailed notifications. It also lets you test your alerts against history for a faster development experience.

Collecting metrics about our systems is fun but what makes a monitoring system useful is alerting when anomalies arise. This is the real strength of Bosun.

Bosun encourages a particular workflow that makes it easy to design, test, and deploy an alert. If you look at the top of the Bosun display, the tabs include Items, Graph, Expression, Rule, and Test config in left-to-right order; that reflects the phases you go through as you create an alert. In general, first you'll select an item (metric) that is the basis of the alert.

SBB License	GNU General Public License (GPL) 2.0
Core Technology	GO
Project URL	http://bosun.org/
Source Location	https://github.com/bosun-monitor/bosun
Tag(s)	Security, SIEM

10.0.6 Cameradar

Cameradar hacks its way into RTSP videosurveillance cameras.

Cameradar allows you to

- **Detect open RTSP hosts** on any accessible target host

- Detect which device model is streaming

- Launch automated dictionary attacks to get their **stream route** (e.g.: `/live.sdp`)

- Launch automated dictionary attacks to get the **username and password** of the cameras

- Retrieve a complete and user-friendly report of the results

SBB License	GNU General Public License (GPL) 2.0
Core Technology	GOlang
Project URL	https://github.com/Ullaakut/cameradar
Source Location	https://github.com/Ullaakut/cameradar
Tag(s)	Security, Test Tool, Vulnerability scanning

10.0.7 CLIP OS

The CLIP OS project is an open source project maintained by the ANSSI (National Cybersecurity Agency of France) that aims to build a secure, multi-level operating system, based on the Linux kernel and a lot of free and open source software.

Documentation can be found on: https://docs.clip-os.org/index.html

SBB License	GNU Lesser General Public License (LGPL) 3.0
Core Technology	C
Project URL	https://clip-os.org/en/
Source Location	https://github.com/CLIPOS/
Tag(s)	Operating System, Security

10.0.8 ClusterFuzz

ClusterFuzz is a scalable fuzzing infrastructure which finds security and stability issues in software.

It is used by Google for fuzzing the Chrome Browser, and serves as the fuzzing backend for OSS-Fuzz.

ClusterFuzz provides many features which help seamlessly integrate fuzzing into a software project's development process:

- Highly scalable. Google's internal instance runs on over 25,000 machines.

- Accurate deduplication of crashes.

- Fully automatic bug filing and closing for issue trackers (Monorail only for now).

- Testcase minimization.

- Regression finding through bisection.

- Statistics for analyzing fuzzer performance, and crash rates.

- Easy to use web interface for management and viewing crashes.

- Support for coverage guided fuzzing (e.g. libFuzzer and AFL) and blackbox fuzzing.

ClusterFuzz is written in Python and Go

SBB License	Apache License 2.0
Core Technology	Python, GO
Project URL	https://github.com/google/clusterfuzz
Source Location	https://github.com/google/clusterfuzz
Tag(s)	Python, Security

10.0.9 Data Seal

Data Seal is a lightweight, UELMA-compliant data authentication service.

Data Seal is a project of U.S. Open Data to provide a system where open data released by governments can be authenticated by end users—whether or not the data was most recently downloaded from the official source.

Government data releases need to abide by local laws (for example, the District of Columbia Official Code) and should also abide by the Uniform Electronic Legal Material Act (UELMA). Part of the UELMA provisions state that "legal material be... authenticated, by providing a method to determine that it is unaltered".

Data Seal provides agencies with a web-based interface to provide this functionality.

SBB License	GNU General Public License (GPL) 2.0
Core Technology	Django/Python
Project URL	https://github.com/unitedstates/data-seal/wiki
Source Location	https://github.com/unitedstates/data-seal
Tag(s)	data authentication, Security

10.0.10 Datastream

An open-source framework for real-time anomaly detection using Python, ElasticSearch and Kiban. Also uses scikit-learn.

SBB License	Apache License 2.0
Core Technology	Python
Project URL	https://github.com/MentatInnovations/datastream.io
Source Location	https://github.com/MentatInnovations/datastream.io
Tag(s)	ML, Monitoring, Security

10.0.11 Deeptracy

Deeptracy scans your project dependencies to spot vulnerabilities. Is a meta tool to analyze the security issues in third party libraries used in your project.

SBB License	Apache License 2.0
Core Technology	Python
Project URL	https://deeptracy.readthedocs.io/en/latest/
Source Location	https://github.com/BBVA/deeptracy
Tag(s)	Security

10.0.12 Diffoscope

Diffoscope will try to get to the bottom of what makes files or directories different. It will recursively unpack archives of many kinds and transform various binary formats into more human readable form to compare them. It can compare two tarballs, ISO images, or PDF just as easily.

It can be scripted through error codes, and a report can be produced with the detected differences. The report can be text or HTML. When no type of report has been selected, diffoscope defaults to write a text report on the standard output.

Diffoscope was initially started by the "reproducible builds" Debian project and now being developed as part of the (wider) "Reproducible Builds" initiative. It is meant to be able to quickly understand why two builds of the same package produce different outputs. diffoscope was previously named debbindiff.

SBB License	GNU General Public License (GPL) 3.0
Core Technology	Python, CPP
Project URL	https://diffoscope.org/
Source Location	https://salsa.debian.org/reproducible-builds/diffoscope
Tag(s)	Security

10.0.13 Duplicity

Duplicity backs directories by producing encrypted tar-format volumes and uploading them to a remote or local file server.

SBB License	GNU General Public License (GPL) 3.0
Core Technology	Python
Project URL	http://duplicity.nongnu.org/
Source Location	https://code.launchpad.net/duplicity
Tag(s)	backup, Security

10.0.14 Evilginx2

Standalone man-in-the-middle attack framework used for phishing login credentials along with session cookies, allowing for the bypass of 2-factor authentication.

This tool is a successor to Evilginx, released in 2017, which used a custom version of nginx HTTP server to provide man-in-the-middle functionality to act as a proxy between a browser and phished website. Present version is fully written in GO as a standalone application, which implements its own HTTP and DNS server, making it extremely easy to set up and use.

SBB License	GNU General Public License (GPL) 3.0
Core Technology	GO
Project URL	https://github.com/kgretzky/evilginx2
Source Location	https://github.com/kgretzky/evilginx2
Tag(s)	Security, Vulnerability scanning

10.0.15 Fail2ban

Fail2ban scans log files (e.g. `/var/log/apache/error_log`) and bans IPs that show the malicious signs — too many password failures, seeking for exploits, etc. Generally Fail2Ban is then used to update firewall rules to reject the IP addresses for a specified amount of time, although any arbitrary other **action** (e.g. sending an email) could also be configured. Out of the box Fail2Ban comes with **filters** for various services (apache, courier, ssh, etc).

SBB License	GNU General Public License (GPL) 2.0
Core Technology	Python
Project URL	https://www.fail2ban.org/wiki/index.php/Main_Page
Source Location	https://github.com/fail2ban
Tag(s)	Network, network diagnostic, Python, Security

10.0.16 FIDO (Fully Integrated Defense Operation)

FIDO (Fully Integrated Defense Operation – apologies to the FIDO Alliance for acronym collision) is developed by NetFlix and is now OSS. This system is for automatically analyzing security events and responding to security incidents.

The premise of FIDO is simple... each year companies are receiving an ever increasing amount of security related alerts. Instead of hiring more analyst to comb through the endless stream of alerts we automate the analysis to combat the barrage of information. Simply put, we integrate and then automate the manual human processes by codifying the logic and process used by threat analysts to provide consistent and reliable results.

The typical process for investigating security-related alerts is labor intensive and largely manual. To make the situation more difficult, as attacks increase in number and diversity, there is an increasing array of detection systems deployed and generating even more alerts for security teams to investigate.

FIDO is a NetFlix OSS project, see: http://techblog.netflix.com/2015/05/introducing-fido-automated-security.html

SBB License	Apache License 2.0
Core Technology	C#
Project URL	https://github.com/Netflix/Fido/wiki
Source Location	https://github.com/Netflix/Fido
Tag(s)	Security, SIEM

10.0.17 FourOneOne

411 is An Alert Management Web Application. If offers:

- A Search scheduler.Configure Searches to periodically run against a variety of data sources. You can define a custom pipeline of Filters to manipulate any generated Alerts and forward them to multiple Targets.

- An alert management interface.Review and manage Alerts through the web interface. You can apply renderers to alerts to enrich them with additional metadata.

Typical Use cases for 411:

- You want to detect when certain log lines show up in ES.

- You want to detect when a Graphite metric changes.

- You want to detect when a server stops responding

- You want to manage alerts through a simple workflow. And much more!

A working demo is available at https://demo.fouroneone.io/

SBB License	MIT License
Core Technology	PHP
Project URL	' <>'__
Source Location	https://github.com/etsy/411
Tag(s)	Alerting, Loganalyze, Security

10.0.18 Ghidra

Ghidra is a software reverse engineering (SRE) framework created and maintained by the National Security Agency Research Directorate. This framework includes a suite of full-featured, high-end software analysis tools that enable users to analyze compiled code on a variety of platforms including Windows, macOS, and Linux. Capabilities include disassembly, assembly, decompilation, graphing, and scripting, along with hundreds of other features. Ghidra supports a wide variety of processor instruction sets and executable formats and can be run in both user-interactive and automated modes. Users may also develop their own Ghidra plug-in components and/or scripts using Java or Python.

SBB License	Apache License 2.0
Core Technology	Java
Project URL	https://ghidra-sre.org/
Source Location	https://github.com/NationalSecurityAgency/ghidra
Tag(s)	Security, Test Tool

10.0.19 GNUnet

GNUnet is a mesh routing layer for end-to-end encrypted networking and a framework for distributed applications designed to replace the old insecure Internet protocol stack.

In other words, GNUnet provides a strong foundation of free software for a global, distributed network that provides security and privacy. Along with an application for secure publication of files, it has grown to include all kinds of basic applications for the foundation of a GNU internet.

GNUnet is an official GNU package.

The foremost goal of the GNUnet project is to become a widely used, reliable, open, non-discriminating, egalitarian, unfettered and censorship-resistant system of free information exchange. We value free speech above state secrets, law-enforcement or intellectual property. GNUnet is supposed to be an anarchistic network, where the only limitation for peers is that they must contribute enough back to the network such that their resource consumption does not have a significant impact on other users. GNUnet should be more than just another file-sharing network. The plan is to offer many other services and in particular to serve as a development platform for the next generation of decentralized Internet protocols.

SBB License	GNU General Public License (GPL) 2.0
Core Technology	C
Project URL	https://gnunet.org/
Source Location	https://gnunet.org/svn/
Tag(s)	Privacy, Security

10.0.20 Gophish

Gophish is a powerful, open-source phishing framework that makes it easy to test your organization's exposure to phishing.

SBB License	MIT License
Core Technology	GO
Project URL	https://getgophish.com/
Source Location	https://github.com/gophish/gophish
Tag(s)	Security

10.0.21 Gryffin

Gryffin is a large scale web security scanning platform. Created by Yahoo, and since September 2015 available as open source.

It is not yet another scanner. It was written to solve two specific problems with existing scanners: coverage and scale. Better coverage translates to fewer false negatives. Inherent scalability translates to capability of scanning, and supporting a large elastic application infrastructure. Simply put, the ability to scan 1000 applications today to 100,000 applications tomorrow by straightforward horizontal scaling.

SBB License	MIT License
Core Technology	Go
Project URL	https://github.com/yahoo/gryffin
Source Location	https://github.com/yahoo/gryffin
Tag(s)	IDS, Security, Vulnerability scanning

10.0.22 Hammertime

Hammertime: a software suite for testing, profiling and simulating the rowhammer DRAM defect.

SBB License	GNU General Public License (GPL) 2.0
Core Technology	Python / C
Project URL	https://github.com/vusec/hammertime
Source Location	https://github.com/vusec/hammertime
Tag(s)	Security, Test Tool

10.0.23 Hashcat

Hashcat is the world's fastest and most advanced password recovery utility, supporting five unique modes of attack for over 200 highly-optimized hashing algorithms. hashcat currently supports CPUs, GPUs, and other hardware accelerators on Linux, Windows, and macOS, and has facilities to help enable distributed password cracking.

SBB License	MIT License
Core Technology	C
Project URL	https://hashcat.net/hashcat/
Source Location	https://github.com/hashcat/hashcat
Tag(s)	Password, Security

10.0.24 Httpswatch

Test tool and site to verify if HTTPS is used as should be for website.

SBB License	GNU General Public License (GPL) 2.0
Core Technology	Python
Project URL	https://httpswatch.com
Source Location	https://github.com/benjaminp/httpswatch
Tag(s)	Security, Test Tool

10.0.25 Kali

Kali is the most complete 'Penetration Testing Linux Distribution' around. Everything you need for penetration testing is collected, tested and made available on this linux distribution. Of course all tools are OSS. The complete list of tools can be found here:http://tools.kali.org/ tools-listing

SBB License	GNU General Public License (GPL) 2.0
Core Technology	N.A. (OSS Tool collection)
Project URL	https://www.kali.org/
Source Location	http://git.kali.org/gitweb/
Tag(s)	Security, Sniffer, Vulnerability scanning

10.0.26 Keycloak

Keycloak is an Open Source Identity and Access Management solution for modern Applications and Services.

Users authenticate with Keycloak rather than individual applications. This means that your applications don't have to deal with login forms, authenticating users, and storing users. Once logged-in to Keycloak, users don't have to login again to access a different application.

SBB License	Apache License 2.0
Core Technology	Java
Project URL	https://www.keycloak.org/
Source Location	https://github.com/keycloak/keycloak
Tag(s)	Security

10.0.27 Kismet

Kismet is an 802.11 layer2 wireless network detector, sniffer, and intrusion detection system. Kismet will work with any wireless card which supports raw monitoring (rfmon) mode, and (with appropriate hardware) can sniff 802.11b, 802.11a, 802.11g, and 802.11n traffic. Kismet also supports plugins which allow sniffing other media such as DECT.

Kismet identifies networks by passively collecting packets and detecting standard named networks, detecting (and given time, decloaking) hidden networks, and inferring the presence of non beaconing networks via data traffic. The great feature of Kismet is that this tool works working passively, so detection by IDS is prevented when scanning WLAN's.

SBB License	GNU General Public License (GPL) 2.0
Core Technology	C++
Project URL	http://www.kismetwireless.net/
Source Location	https://www.kismetwireless.net/code/
Tag(s)	IDS, Security, Sniffer

10.0.28 Lascar

Ledger's Advanced Side Channel Analysis Repository

A fast, versatile, and open source python3 library designed to facilitate Side-Channel Analysis. Lascar provides primitives for all the required steps in Side Channel Analysis. It allows the implementaton of end-to-end Side Channel Attacks.

lascar is intended to be used by seasoned side-channel attackers as well as laymen who would like to get a feel of side-channel analysis.

From side-channel acquisitions to results management, passing by signal synchronisation, custom attacks, *lascar* provides classes/functions to solve most of the obstacles an attacker would face, when needed to perform sound, state-of-the-art side-channel analysis.

SBB License	GNU General Public License (GPL) 2.0
Core Technology	Python
Project URL	https://github.com/Ledger-Donjon/lascar
Source Location	https://github.com/Ledger-Donjon/lascar
Tag(s)	Security

10.0.29 Libreswan

Libreswan is an IPsec implementation for Linux. Libreswan is a free software implementation of the most widely supported and standarized VPN protocol based on ("IPsec") and the Internet Key Exchange ("IKE").

SBB License	GNU General Public License (GPL) 2.0
Core Technology	
Project URL	https://libreswan.org/
Source Location	https://github.com/libreswan/libreswan
Tag(s)	communication, Cryptography, Security

10.0.30 Lightbulb

LightBulb is an open source python framework for auditing web applications firewalls.

Project created and started in 2016.

SBB License	MIT License
Core Technology	Python
Project URL	' <> '__
Source Location	https://github.com/lightbulb-framework/ lightbulb-framework
Tag(s)	Audit, Security, Waf

10.0.31 Lynis

Lynis is a suite of tools (shell scripts) for security auditing, compliance and hardening for Linux, Mac OS, and Unix based systems. Of course many (better) audit tools are available, but this one is simple and straightforward. So easy to extend and to improve. Especially if you like shell-scripting.

Michael Boelen from the Netherlands (owner of company cisofy.com) created this software.

SBB License	GNU General Public License (GPL) 3.0
Core Technology	unix-shell scripts
Project URL	https://cisofy.com
Source Location	https://github.com/CISOfy/lynis/
Tag(s)	Audit, Security

10.0.32 Magic Wormhole

Get things from one computer to another, safely.

This package provides a library and a command-line tool named wormhole, which makes it possible to get arbitrary-sized files and directories (or short pieces of text) from one computer to another. The two endpoints are identified by using identical "wormhole codes": in general, the sending machine generates and displays the code, which must then be typed into the receiving machine.

SBB License	MIT License
Core Technology	Python
Project URL	https://magic-wormhole.readthedocs.io/en/latest/
Source Location	https://github.com/warner/magic-wormhole
Tag(s)	Security

10.0.33 Malspider

Malspider is a web spidering framework that detects characteristics of web compromises.

Based on Scrapy framework.

Malspider is a web spidering framework that inspects websites for characteristics of compromise. Malspider has three purposes:

- **Website Integrity Monitoring**: monitor your organization's website (or your personal website) for potentially malicious changes.

- **Generate Threat Intelligence:** keep an eye on previously compromised sites, currently compromised sites, or sites that may be targeted by various threat actors.

- **Validate Web Compromises**: Is this website still compromised?

Malspider has built-in detection for characteristics of compromise like hidden iframes, reconnaisance frameworks, vbscript injection, email address disclosure, etc.

SBB License	BSD License 2.0 (3-clause, New or Revised) License
Core Technology	Python
Project URL	https://github.com/ciscocsirt/malspider
Source Location	https://github.com/ciscocsirt/malspider
Tag(s)	Security, Vulnerability scanning

10.0.34 Mantra

OWASP Mantra is a collection of free and open source tools integrated into a web browser, which can become handy for students, penetration testers, web application developers,security professionals etc. It is portable, ready-to-run, compact and follows the true spirit of free and open source software.

Mantra is lite, flexible, portable and user friendly with a nice graphical user interface. You can carry it in memory cards, flash drives, CD/DVDs, etc. It can be run natively on Linux, Windows and Mac platforms. It can also be installed on to your system within minutes. Mantra is absolutely free of cost and takes no time for you to set up.

Mantra is a browser especially designed for web application security testing. By having such a product, more people will come to know the easiness and flexibility of being able to follow basic testing procedures within the browser. Mantra believes that having such a portable, easy to use and yet powerful platform can be helpful for the industry.

Mantra has many built in tools to modify headers, manipulate input strings, replay GET/POST requests, edit cookies, quickly switch between multiple proxies, control forced redirects etc. This makes it a good software for performing basic security checks and sometimes, exploitation. Thus, Mantra can be used to solve basic levels of various web based CTFs, showcase security issues in vulnerable web applications etc.

SBB License	GNU General Public License (GPL) 3.0
Core Technology	javascript
Project URL	http://www.getmantra.com
Source Location	https://code.google.com/p/getmantra/
Tag(s)	Security, Test Tool

10.0.35 MITMEngine

The goal of this project is to allow for accurate detection of HTTPS interception and robust TLS fingerprinting. This project is based off of The Security Impact of HTTPS Interception, and started as a port to Go of their processing scripts and fingerprints.

In a basic HTTPS connection, a browser (client) establishes a TLS connection directly to an origin server to send requests and download content. However, many connections on the Internet are not directly from a browser to the server serving the website, but instead traverse through some type of proxy or middlebox (a "monster-in-the-middle" or MITM). There are many reasons for this behavior, both malicious and benign.

SBB License	BSD License 2.0 (3-clause, New or Revised) License
Core Technology	GO
Project URL	https://blog.cloudflare.com/monsters-in-the-middleboxes/
Source Location	https://github.com/cloudflare/mitmengine
Tag(s)	Security, Test Tool

10.0.36 Mitmproxy

An interactive SSL-capable intercepting HTTP proxy for penetration testers and software developers. Console program that allows traffic flows to be intercepted, inspected, modified and replayed.

Part of mitmproxy is **mitmdump** is the command-line companion to mitmproxy. It provides tcpdump-like functionality to let you view, record, and programmatically transform HTTP traffic. See the `--help` flag output for complete documentation.

SBB License	MIT License
Core Technology	Python
Project URL	https://mitmproxy.org
Source Location	https://github.com/mitmproxy/mitmproxy
Tag(s)	HTTP Proxy, Privacy, Security, Sniffer

10.0.37 ModSecurity

ModSecurity is an open source, cross-platform web application firewall (WAF) module. Known as the "Swiss Army Knife" of WAFs, it enables web application defenders to gain visibility into HTTP(S) traffic and provides a power rules language and API to implement advanced protections.

ModSecurity is an open source, cross platform web application firewall (WAF) engine for Apache, IIS and Nginx that is developed by Trustwave's SpiderLabs. It has a robust event-based programming language which provides protection from a range of attacks against web applications and allows for HTTP traffic monitoring, logging and real-time analyse.

SBB License	Apache License 2.0
Core Technology	C
Project URL	http://www.modsecurity.org/
Source Location	https://github.com/SpiderLabs/ModSecurity
Tag(s)	Security, Waf

10.0.38 MOSP

A platform to create, edit and share JSON Security objects.

The goal of this platform is to gather security related JSON schemas and objects. You can use any available schemas in order to create shareable JSON objects. It also possible to keep an object private even if our goal is to promote the sharing of information. JSON schemas are always public.

All content is licensed under CC-BY-SA.

Integration with third-party applications is possible thanks to an API:

- JSON Schemas

- JSON Objects

SBB License	GNU Affero General Public License Version 3
Core Technology	JSON
Project URL	http://objects.monarc.lu/
Source Location	https://github.com/CASES-LU/MOSP
Tag(s)	JSON, Security

10.0.39 Mozilla HTTP Observatory

The Mozilla HTTP Observatory is a set of tools to analyze your website and inform you if you are utilizing the many available methods to secure it.

SBB License	Mozilla Public License (MPL) 1.1
Core Technology	Python
Project URL	https://observatory.mozilla.org/
Source Location	https://github.com/mozilla/http-observatory
Tag(s)	Python, Security, Vulnerability scanning

10.0.40 Mythril

Mythril is a security analysis tool for Ethereum smart contracts. It uses the LASER-ethereum symbolic virtual machine to detect various types of issues. Use it to analyze source code or as a nmap-style black-box blockchain scanner (an "ethermap" if you will).

SBB License	MIT License
Core Technology	Python
Project URL	https://github.com/ConsenSys/mythril
Source Location	https://github.com/ConsenSys/mythril
Tag(s)	BlockChain, Security

10.0.41 OpenVAS

OpenVAS is a framework of several services and tools offering a comprehensive and powerful vulnerability scanning and vulnerability management solution.

The core of this SSL-secured service-oriented architecture is the **OpenVAS Scanner**. The scanner very efficiently executes the actual Network Vulnerability Tests (NVTs) which are served with daily updates via the OpenVAS NVT Feed or via a commercial feed service.

SBB License	GNU General Public License (GPL) 2.0
Core Technology	C
Project URL	http://www.openvas.org
Source Location	https://scm.wald.intevation.org/svn/openvas/trunk
Tag(s)	Security, Vulnerability scanning

10.0.42 ORY Hydra

ORY Hydra is a hardened OAuth2 and OpenID Connect server optimized for low-latency, high throughput, and low resource consumption. ORY Hydra is not an identity provider (user sign up, user log in, password reset flow), but connects to your existing identity provider through a consent app.

SBB License	Apache License 2.0
Core Technology	GOlang
Project URL	https://www.ory.sh/
Source Location	https://github.com/ory/hydra
Tag(s)	Security

10.0.43 osquery

SQL powered operating system instrumentation, monitoring, and analytics. Osquery exposes an operating system as a high-performance relational database. This allows you to write SQL-based queries to explore operating system data. With osquery, SQL tables represent abstract concepts such as running processes, loaded kernel modules, open network connections, browser plugins, hardware events or file hashes.

Developed by Facebook.

SBB License	GNU General Public License (GPL) 2.0
Core Technology	C
Project URL	https://osquery.io/
Source Location	https://github.com/facebook/osquery
Tag(s)	Loganalyze, Monitoring, Security

10.0.44 OWASP ZCR Shellcoder

OWASP ZCR Shellcoder is an open source software in python language which lets you generate customized shellcodes for various operation systems. Shellcodesare small codes in assembly which could be use as the payload in software exploiting. Other usages are in malwares, bypassing antiviruses, obfuscated codes and etc.

SBB License	GNU General Public License (GPL) 3.0
Core Technology	Python
Project URL	https://www.owasp org/index.php/OWASP_ZSC_Tool_Project
Source Location	https://github.com/Ali-Razmjoo/OWASP-ZSC/
Tag(s)	Security, Test Tool

10.0.45 OWASP Zed Attack Proxy (ZAP)

The OWASP Zed Attack Proxy (ZAP) is an easy to use integrated penetration testing tool for finding vulnerabilities in web applications.

It is designed to be used by people with a wide range of security experience and as such is ideal for developers and functional testers who are new to penetration testing as well as being a useful addition to an experienced pen testers toolbox.

SBB License	Apache License 2.0
Core Technology	Java
Project URL	https://www.owasp.org/index.php/OWASP_Zed_Attack_Proxy_Project#tab=Main
Source Location	https://github.com/zaproxy/zaproxy
Tag(s)	Security

10.0.46 Phpseclib (PHP Secure Communications Library)

Phpseclib is designed to be ultra-compatible. It works on PHP4+ (PHP4, assuming the use of PHP_Compat) and doesn't require any extensions. For purposes of speed, **mcrypt is used** if it's available **as is gmp or bcmath** (in that order), but they are not required. Phpseclib is designed to be fully interoperable with OpenSSL and other standardized cryptography programs and protocols.

Phpseclib is a pure-PHP implementations of:

- BigIntegers
- RSA
- SSH2
- SFTP
- X.509
- Symmetric key encryption

    - AES
    - Rijndael
    - Twofish
    - Blowfish
    - DES
    - 3DES
    - RC4
    - RC2

SBB License	MIT License
Core Technology	PHP
Project URL	http://phpseclib.sourceforge.net/
Source Location	https://github.com/phpseclib/phpseclib
Tag(s)	Cryptography, Security

10.0.47 Pysyft

A library for encrypted, privacy preserving deep learning. PySyft is a Python library for secure, private Deep Learning. PySyft decouples private data from model training, using Multi-Party Computation (MPC) within PyTorch. View the paper on Arxiv.

SBB License	Apache License 2.0
Core Technology	Python
Project URL	https://github.com/OpenMined/PySyft
Source Location	https://github.com/OpenMined/PySyft
Tag(s)	Python, Security

10.0.48 Radare

Unix-like reverse engineering framework and commandline tools.

Radare is a portable reversing framework that can:

- Disassemble (and assemble for) many different architectures

- Debug with local native and remote debuggers (gdb, rap, webui, r2pipe, winedbg, windbg)

- Run on Linux, *BSD, Windows, OSX, Android, iOS, Solaris and Haiku

- Perform forensics on filesystems and data carving

- Be scripted in Python, Javascript, Go and more

- Support collaborative analysis using the embedded webserver

- Visualize data structures of several file types

- Patch programs to uncover new features or fix vulnerabilities

- Use powerful analysis capabilities to speed up reversing

- Aid in software exploitation

SBB License	GNU General Public License (GPL) 3.0
Core Technology	C
Project URL	http://rada.re/r/index.html
Source Location	https://github.com/radare/radare2
Tag(s)	Debugger, Security, software development, Vulnerability scanning

10.0.49 Requests: HTTP for Humans

Requests is the only *Non-GMO* HTTP library for Python, safe for human consumption.

Requests allows you to send *organic, grass-fed* HTTP/1.1 requests, without the need for manual labor. There's no need to manually add query strings to your URLs, or to form-encode your POST data. Keep-alive and HTTP connection pooling are 100% automatic, powered by urllib3, which is embedded within Requests.

SBB License	Apache License 2.0
Core Technology	Python
Project URL	' <>'__
Source Location	https://github.com/kennethreitz/requests
Tag(s)	Security, software development, Test Tool

10.0.50 RIPS (code analyser)

RIPS is a tool written in PHP to find vulnerabilities in PHP applications using static code analysis. By tokenizing and parsing all source code files RIPS is able to transform PHP source code into a program model and to detect sensitive sinks (potentially vulnerable functions) that can be tainted by userinput (influenced by a malicious user) during the program flow. Besides the structured output of found vulnerabilities RIPS also offers an integrated code audit framework for further manual analysis.

RIPS was released during the Month of PHP Security (www.php-security.org).

Features

- detect XSS, SQLi, File disclosure, LFI/RFI, RCE vulnerabilities and more

- 5 verbosity levels for debugging your scan results

- mark vulnerable lines in source code viewer

- highlight variables in the code viewer

- user-defined function code by mouse-over on detected call

- active jumping between function declaration and calls

- list of all user-defined functions (defines and calls), program entry points (user input) and scanned files (with includes) connected to the source code viewer

- graph visualization for files and includes as well as functions and calls

- create CURL exploits for detected vulnerabilities with few clicks

- visualization, description, example, PoC, patch and securing function list for every vulnerability

- 7 different syntax highlighting colour schemata

- display scan result in form of a top-down flow or bottom-up trace

- only minimal requirement is a local web server with PHP and a browser (tested with Firefox)

- regex search function

SBB License	GNU General Public License (GPL) 3.0
Core Technology	PHP
Project URL	http://rips-scanner.sourceforge.net/
Source Location	http://sourceforge.net/projects/rips-scanner/
Tag(s)	Code Analyzer, Security

10.0.51 RouterSploit

The RouterSploit Framework is an open-source exploitation framework dedicated to embedded devices.

It consists of various modules that aids penetration testing operations:

- exploits – modules that take advantage of identified vulnerabilities

- creds – modules designed to test credentials against network services

- scanners – modules that check if target is vulnerable to any exploit

SBB License	GNU General Public License (GPL) 2.0
Core Technology	Python
Project URL	https://github.com/reverse-shell/routersploit
Source Location	https://github.com/reverse-shell/routersploit
Tag(s)	Security, Vulnerability scanning

10.0.52 SecLists

SecLists is the security tester's companion. It is a collection of multiple types of lists used during security assessments. List types include usernames, passwords, URLs, sensitive data grep strings, fuzzing payloads, and many more.

This is an OWASP project (incubator) .

SBB License	MIT License
Core Technology	n.a.
Project URL	https://www.owasp.org/index.php/OWASP_SecLists_Project
Source Location	https://github.com/danielmiessler/SecLists
Tag(s)	Security, Test Tool

10.0.53 Security Monkey

Security Monkey monitors policy changes and alerts on insecure configurations in an AWS account. While Security Monkey's main purpose is security, it also proves a useful tool for tracking down potential problems as it is essentially a change tracking system.

More information: http://techblog.netflix.com/2014/06/announcing-security-monkey-aws-security.html

SBB License	Apache License 2.0
Core Technology	Python
Project URL	http://securitymonkey.readthedocs.org/en/latest/
Source Location	https://github.com/Netflix/security_monkey
Tag(s)	Security, SIEM

10.0.54 SigPloit

SigPloit a signaling security testing framework dedicated to Telecom Security professionals and reasearchers to pentest and exploit vulnerabilites in the signaling protocols used in mobile operators regardless of the geneartion being in use. SigPloit aims to cover all used protocols used in the operators interconnects SS7, GTP (3G), Diameter (4G) or even SIP for IMS and VoLTE infrastructures used in the access layer and SS7 message encapsulation into SIP-T. Recommendations for each vulnerability will be provided to guide the tester and the operator the steps that should be done to enhance their security posture

SBB License	MIT License
Core Technology	Python
Project URL	https://github.com/SigPloiter/SigPloit
Source Location	https://github.com/SigPloiter/SigPloit
Tag(s)	pentest, Security

10.0.55 SIMP (The System Integrity Management Platform)

SIMP is a framework that aims to provide a reasonable combination of security compliance and operational flexibility. Fundamentally, SIMP is a framework that is designed to be secure from a practical point of view out of the box. As a framework, SIMP is designed to be flexed to meet the needs of the end user.

The ultimate goal of the project is to provide a complete management environment focused on compliance with the various profiles in the SCAP Security Guide Project and industry best practice.

Though it is fully capable out of the box, the intent of SIMP is to be molded to your target environment in such a way that deviations are easily identifiable to both Operations Teams and Security Officers. This project is released to the public by the US National Security Agency.

SBB License	MIT License
Core Technology	
Project URL	https://github.com/NationalSecurityAgency/SIMP
Source Location	https://github.com/simp
Tag(s)	Audit, Security

10.0.56 Simplify

Simplify uses a virtual machine to understand what an app does. Then, it applies optimizations to create code that behaves identically, but is easier for a human to understand. Specifically, it takes Smali files as input and outputs a Dex file with (hopefully) identical semantics but less complicated structure.

For example, if an app's strings are encrypted, Simplify will interpret the app in its own virtual machine to determine semantics. Then, it uses the apps own code to decrypt the strings and replaces the encrypted strings and the decryption method calls with the decrypted versions. It's a **generic** deobfuscator because Simplify doesn't need to know how the decryption works ahead of time. This technique also works well for eliminating different types of white noise, such as no-ops and useless arithmetic.

SBB License	MIT License
Core Technology	
Project URL	' <>'__
Source Location	https://github.com/CalebFenton/simplify
Tag(s)	Code Analyzer, Security

10.0.57 Sonarqube

OWASP project. SonarQube provides the capability to not only show health of an application but also to highlight issues newly introduced. With a Quality Gate in place, you can fix the leak and therefore improve code quality systematically.

SonarQube® software (previously called Sonar) is an open source quality management platform, dedicated to continuously analyze and measure technical quality, from project portfolio to method. If you wish to extend the SonarQube platform with open source plugins, have a look at our plugin library.

SBB License	GNU Lesser General Public License (LGPL) 3.0
Core Technology	Java
Project URL	https://www.sonarqube.org/
Source Location	https://github.com/SonarSource/sonarqube
Tag(s)	Security, Vulnerability scanning

10.0.58 SpiderFoot

SpiderFoot is an open source intelligence automation tool. Its goal is to automate the process of gathering intelligence about a given target, which may be an IP address, domain name, hostname or network subnet.

SpiderFoot can be used offensively, i.e. as part of a black-box penetration test to gather information about the target or defensively to identify what information your organisation is freely providing for attackers to use against you.

SBB License	GNU General Public License (GPL) 2.0
Core Technology	Python
Project URL	https://www.spiderfoot.net/
Source Location	https://github.com/smicallef/spiderfoot
Tag(s)	pentest, Python, Security, Test Tool, Vulnerability scanning

10.0.59 Streisand

Streisand is software for setting up secure connections with your friends. A bit like TOR.

Streisand is open source software that sets up a communication server that can run:

- WireGuard

- OpenConnect

- OpenSSH

- OpenVPN

- Shadowsocks

- SSHLH

- Stunnel, or a

- Tor bridge.

After configuration Streisand generates custom instructions to use the communication service chosen. At the end of the run you are given an HTML file with instructions that can be shared with friends, family members, and fellow activists. Setting up Streisand requires still some good Unix knowledge for installation and configuration. So it is a bit of a hassle. (status 2018)

Using Streisand reduces the barrier of entry to running a VPN/censorship-bypass server for friends and family and makes secure communication available to more people.

SBB License	GNU General Public License (GPL) 3.0
Core Technology	Python
Project URL	https://github.com/jlund/streisand
Source Location	https://github.com/jlund/streisand
Tag(s)	communication, Privacy, Security

10.0.60 Stunnel

Stunnel is a proxy designed to add TLS encryption functionality to existing clients and servers without any changes in the programs' code. Its architecture is optimized for security, portability, and scalability (including load-balancing), making it suitable for large deployments.

Stunnel uses the OpenSSL library for cryptography, so it supports whatever cryptographic algorithms are compiled into the library. It can benefit from the FIPS 140-2 validation of the OpenSSL FIPS Object Module, as long as the building process meets its Security Policy.

SBB License	GNU General Public License (GPL) 2.0
Core Technology	C
Project URL	https://www.stunnel.org/index.html
Source Location	http://www.usenix.org.uk/mirrors/stunnel/
Tag(s)	Cryptography, Security

10.0.61 Suricata

Suricata is a high performance Network IDS, IPS and Network Security Monitoring engine. Open Source and owned by a community run non-profit foundation, the Open Information Security Foundation (OISF). Suricata is developed by the OISF and its supporting vendors.

SBB License	GNU General Public License (GPL) 2.0
Core Technology	C
Project URL	http://suricata-ids.org
Source Location	https://github.com/inliniac/suricata
Tag(s)	IDS, Security

10.0.62 Susanoo

Susanoo is a REST API security testing framework. Features:

- Configurable inputs/outputs formats

- API Vulnerability Scan: Normal scanning engine that scans for IDOR, Authentication issues, SQL injections, Error stacks.

- Smoke Scan: Custom output checks for known pocs can be configured to run daily.

SBB License	MIT License
Core Technology	Python
Project URL	https://github.com/ant4g0nist/Susanoo
Source Location	https://github.com/ant4g0nist/Susanoo
Tag(s)	Security, Test Tool

10.0.63 SWAMP (Software Assurance Marketplace)

This security application is a SAAS solution. However it is built of OSS building blocks and available to be use under an friendly OSS license for everyone.

- Capabilities of the SWAMP

- Static analysis

- Operates on the original source code

- Tracks problems down to the location in the original code

- Relatively quick and easy to use

- Provides complete code coverage

- Compare results from multiple tools

- Find and visualize overlaps

- Correlate results

Languages supported: C/C++,Java source, Java bytecode, Python, Ruby. PHP and Javascript are on the roadmap for end 2015 to be supported.

SBB License	GNU General Public License (GPL) 3.0
Core Technology	
Project URL	https://www.mir-swamp.org
Source Location	' <>'__
Tag(s)	Code Analyzer, Security

10.0.64 Tamper Chrome

Tamper Chrome is a Chrome extension that allows you to modify HTTP requests on the fly and aid on web security testing. Tamper Chrome works across all operating systems (including Chrome OS).

SBB License	Apache License 2.0
Core Technology	Javascript
Project URL	https://github.com/google/tamperchrome
Source Location	https://github.com/google/tamperchrome
Tag(s)	Audit, Security, Test Tool

10.0.65 Threat Dragon

Threat Dragon is a free, open-source threat modelling tool from OWASP.

Threat Dragon is an online threat modelling web application including system diagramming and a rule engine to auto-generate threats/mitigations. The focus will be on great UX a powerful rule engine and alignment with other development lifecycle tools.

ThreatDragon is a Single Page Application (SPA) using Angular on the client and node.js on the server.

Thread Dragon is currently in alfa stage.

SBB License	MIT License
Core Technology	Javascript / NodeJS
Project URL	https://www.owasp.org/index.php/OWASP_Threat_Dragon
Source Location	https://github.com/mike-goodwin/owasp-threat-dragon
Tag(s)	Modelling, Security

10.0.66 Tink

Tink provides secure APIs that are easy to use correctly and hard(er) to misuse. It reduces common crypto pitfalls with user-centered design, careful implementation and code reviews, and extensive testing. At Google, Tink is already being used to secure data of many products such as AdMob, Google Pay, Google Assistant, Firebase, the Android Search App, etc.

SBB License	Apache License 2.0
Core Technology	Java
Project URL	https://github.com/google/tink
Source Location	https://github.com/google/tink
Tag(s)	Cryptography, Security

10.0.67 Tlsfuzzer

TLS test suite and fuzze. Fuzzer and test suite for TLS (v1.0, v1.1, v1.2) implementations.

tlsfuzzer verifies only TLS level behaviour, it does not perform any checks on the certificate (like hostname validation, CA signatures or key usage). It does however verify if the signatures made on TLS message by the server (like in Server Key Exchange message) match the certificate sent by the server.

SBB License	GNU General Public License (GPL) 2.0
Core Technology	Python
Project URL	https://github.com/tomato42/tlsfuzzer
Source Location	https://github.com/tomato42/tlsfuzzer
Tag(s)	Audit, Security, Test Tool

10.0.68 Tor

Tor is free software and an open network that helps you defend against traffic analysis, a form of network surveillance that threatens personal freedom and privacy, confidential business activities and relationships, and state security. Creating your own Tor network is easy with this software, or use existing Tor nodes.

SBB License	GNU General Public License (GPL) 2.0
Core Technology	
Project URL	https://www.torproject.org
Source Location	https://www.torproject.org/dist/
Tag(s)	Cryptography, Privacy, Security

10.0.69 Unfurl

An Entropy-Based Link Vulnerability Analysis Tool.

unfurl is a screening tool for automating URL entropy analysis. The big idea is to find tokens in a large list of URLs that have low entropy. These might be susceptible to brute force attacks.

SBB License	GNU General Public License (GPL) 2.0
Core Technology	Python
Project URL	https://jlospinoso.github.io/python/unfurl/abrade/ hacking/2018/02/08/unfurl-url-analysis.html
Source Location	https://github.com/JLospinoso/unfurl
Tag(s)	Security

10.0.70 URL Abuse

URL Abuse is a versatile free software for URL review, analysis and black-list reporting. URL Abuse is composed of a web interface where requests are submitted asynchronously and a back-end system to process the URLs into features modules.

Features:

- HTTP redirects analysis and follows
- Google Safe-Browsing lookup
- Phishtank lookup
- VirusTotal lookup and submission
- URL query lookup
- CIRCL Passive DNS lookup
- CIRCL Passive SSL lookup
- Universal WHOIS lookup for abuse contact
- Sphinx search interface to RT/RTIR ticketing systems. The functionality is disabled by default but can be used to display information about existing report of malicious URLs.

Please note that some of the API services will require an API key. The API keys should be located in the root of the URL Abuse directory. There is also an online version to use: https://www.circl.lu/urlabuse/

SBB License	GNU Affero General Public License Version 3
Core Technology	Python
Project URL	http://www.circl.lu/services/urlabuse/
Source Location	https://github.com/CIRCL/url-abuse
Tag(s)	Python, Security

10.0.71 Vault

Vault is a tool for securely accessing secrets. A secret is anything that you want to tightly control access to, such as API keys, passwords, certificates, and more. Vault provides a unified interface to any secret, while providing tight access control and recording a detailed audit log.

Vault secures, stores, and tightly controls access to tokens, passwords, certificates, API keys, and other secrets in modern computing. Vault handles leasing, key revocation, key rolling, and auditing. Vault presents a unified API to access multiple backends: HSMs, AWS IAM, SQL databases, raw key/value, and more.

A modern system requires access to a multitude of secrets: database credentials, API keys for external services, credentials for service-oriented architecture communication, etc. Understanding who is accessing what secrets is already very difficult and platform-specific. Adding on key rolling, secure storage, and detailed audit logs is almost impossible without a custom solution. This is where Vault steps in.

SBB License	Mozilla Public License (MPL) 1.1
Core Technology	GO
Project URL	https://vaultproject.io
Source Location	https://github.com/hashicorp/vault
Tag(s)	Security

10.0.72 VERIS

VERIS The Vocabulary for Event Recording and Incident Sharing.

The Vocabulary for Event Recording and Incident Sharing (VERIS) is a set of metrics designed to provide a common language for describing security incidents in a structured and repeatable manner. VERIS is a response to one of the most critical and persistent challenges in the security industry – a lack of quality information. VERIS targets this problem by helping organizations to collect useful incident-related information and to share that information – anonymously and responsibly – with others.

SBB License	GNU General Public License (GPL) 2.0
Core Technology	Python
Project URL	http://veriscommunity.net/index.html
Source Location	https://github.com/vz-risk/veris
Tag(s)	Security

10.0.73 VSAQ: Vendor Security Assessment Questionnaire

VSAQ is an interactive questionnaire application. Its initial purpose was to support security reviews by facilitating not only the collection of information, but also the redisplay of collected data in templated form.

At Google, questionnaires like the ones in this repository are used to assess the security programs of third parties. But the templates provided can be used for a variety of purposes, including doing a self-assessment of your own security program, or simply becoming familiar with issues affecting the security of web applications.

SBB License	Apache License 2.0
Core Technology	Javascript
Project URL	https://vsaq-demo.withgoogle.com/
Source Location	https://github.com/google/vsaq
Tag(s)	Audit, Questionnaire, Security

10.0.74 w3af (Web Application Attack and Audit Framework)

w3af is a Web Application Attack and Audit Framework. The project's goal is to create a framework to help you secure your web applications by finding and exploiting all web application vulnerabilities.

The w3af framework is divided into three main sections:

1. The core, which coordinates the whole process and provides libraries for using in plugins.

2. The user interfaces, which allow the user to configure and start scans

3. The plugins, which find links and vulnerabilities

SBB License	GNU General Public License (GPL) 2.0
Core Technology	Phython
Project URL	http://w3af.org/
Source Location	https://github.com/andresriancho/w3af/
Tag(s)	Audit, Security, Test Tool

10.0.75 Wapiti

Wapiti allows you to audit the security of your websites or web applications.

It performs "black-box" scans (it does not study the source code) of the web application by crawling the webpages of the deployed webapp, looking for scripts and forms where it can inject data.

Once it gets the list of URLs, forms and their inputs, Wapiti acts like a fuzzer, injecting payloads to see if a script is vulnerable.

SBB License	GNU General Public License (GPL) 2.0
Core Technology	Python
Project URL	http://wapiti.sourceforge.net/
Source Location	http://wapiti.sourceforge.net/
Tag(s)	Security, Vulnerability scanning

10.0.76 Wifite 2

A complete re-write of wifite, a Python script for auditing wireless networks.

Wifite is an automated wireless attack tool. Wifite was designed for use with pentesting distributions of Linux, such as Kali Linux, Pentoo, Back-Box; any Linux distributions with wireless drivers patched for injection. The script appears to also operate with Ubuntu 11/10, Debian 6, and Fedora 16.

SBB License	GNU General Public License (GPL) 2.0
Core Technology	Python
Project URL	https://github.com/derv82/wifite2
Source Location	https://github.com/derv82/wifite2
Tag(s)	Audit, pentest, Security

10.0.77 WireGuard

WireGuard is an extremely simple yet fast and modern VPN that utilizes state-of-the-art cryptography. It aims to be faster, simpler, leaner, and more useful than IPSec, while avoiding the massive headache. It intends to be considerably more performant than OpenVPN. WireGuard is designed as a general purpose VPN for running on embedded interfaces and super computers alike, fit for many different circumstances. Initially released for the Linux kernel, it plans to be cross-platform and widely deployable. It is currently under heavy development, but already it might be regarded as the most secure, easiest to use, and simplest VPN solution in the industry.

SBB License	GNU General Public License (GPL) 2.0
Core Technology	C
Project URL	https://www.wireguard.com/
Source Location	https://git.zx2c4.com/WireGuard/
Tag(s)	Privacy, Security, VPN

10.0.78 YARA

YARA is a tool aimed at (but not limited to) helping malware researchers to identify and classify malware samples. With YARA you can create descriptions of malware families (or whatever you want to describe) based on textual or binary patterns.

SBB License	MIT License
Core Technology	C
Project URL	https://virustotal.github.io/yara/
Source Location	https://github.com/virustotal/yara
Tag(s)	Malware, Security

10.0.79 Zeek

Zeek is a powerful framework for network analysis and security monitoring.

(Zeek is the new name for the long-established Bro system. Note that parts of the system retain the "Bro" name, and it also often appears in the documentation and distributions.)

SBB License	GNU General Public License (GPL) 2.0
Core Technology	C
Project URL	https://www.zeek.org/
Source Location	https://github.com/zeek/zeek
Tag(s)	IDS, Security

End of SBB list

ELEVEN

OSS PRIVACY APPLICATIONS

11.0.1 About this list

We know we can never be complete with an overview of OSS privacy applications. Good privacy solution building blocks are not wide spread available. This is due to the fact that the old fashioned business model of tracking users and user activity should never ever be possible. So for communication there is Tor or create your own decentralized device and encrypted protocol. You can find a lot of tools that make it real simple to build a real private communication channel.

Note:An up-to-date list is always online.

Criteria used for products mentioned in this chapter are equal as for security solutions:

- The products must have a valid OSS license;

- The project must be active and must meet a certain quality level;

- The product must be in use somewhere (*)

(*) Unfortunately we can and never will expose information where products are in use, however many mature products have solid references on their website, along with active user groups.

11.0.2 Amiunique

Amiunique has shares some goals with panoticlick, but it provides a number of novelties:

- amiunique implements the most recent techniques for fingerprinting, including webGL and canvas

- amiunique provides more information to the users, including global statistics, as well as a concise summary of the main characteristics of a browser

created and maintained by a team of researchers, who investigates the software monocultures and software diversity on the web. The research team is financially supported by the DIVERSIFY European project and by a grant from the INSA-Rennes school.

SBB License	GNU General Public License (GPL) 2.0
Core Technology	Java
Project URL	https://amiunique.org/
Source Location	https://github.com/DIVERSIFY-project/amiunique
Tag(s)	fingerprinting, Privacy

11.0.3 Blockstack

Blockstack is a new decentralized internet where users own their data and apps run locally. A browser portal is all that's needed to get started.

With Blockstack, users control their data and apps run on their devices. There are no middlemen, no passwords, no massive data silos to breach, and no services tracking us around the internet.

The applications on blockstack are server-less and decentralized. Developers start by building a single-page application in Javascript, Then, instead of plugging the frontend into a centralized API, they plug into an API run by the user. Developers install a library called 'blockstack.js' and don't have to worry about running servers, maintaining databases, or building out user management systems.

SBB License	GNU General Public License (GPL) 3.0
Core Technology	Python + Javascript
Project URL	https://blockstack.org
Source Location	https://github.com/blockstack
Tag(s)	Privacy

11.0.4 BRIAR

Secure messaging, anywhere:

- Peer-to-peer encrypted messaging and forums

- Messages are stored securely on your device, not in the cloud

- Connect directly with nearby contacts – no Internet access required

- Free and open source software

SBB License	GNU General Public License (GPL) 3.0
Core Technology	Java
Project URL	https://briarproject.org/index.html
Source Location	https://code.briarproject.org/akwizgran/briar/tree/master
Tag(s)	Messaging, Privacy

11.0.5 ChatSecure

ChatSecure is a free and open source messaging app that features OTR encryption over XMPP. You can connect to your existing accounts on Facebook or Google, create new accounts on public XMPP servers (including via Tor), or even connect to your own server for extra security.

SBB License	Mozilla Public License (MPL) 1.1
Core Technology	Objective C
Project URL	https://chatsecure.org
Source Location	https://github.com/ChatSecure
Tag(s)	Chat, Privacy

11.0.6 Diaspora

A privacy-aware, distributed, open source social network.

SBB License	GNU Affero General Public License Version 3
Core Technology	Ruby
Project URL	https://diasporafoundation.org/
Source Location	https://github.com/diaspora/diaspora
Tag(s)	communication, Privacy

11.0.7 Fingerprintjs2

Modern & flexible browser fingerprinting library. Also used as demo on EFF.org site.

SBB License	GNU General Public License (GPL) 2.0
Core Technology	Javascript
Project URL	http://valve.github.io/fingerprintjs2/
Source Location	https://github.com/Valve/fingerprintjs2
Tag(s)	fingerprinting, Privacy

11.0.8 FreedomBox

FreedomBox is a 100% free software self-hosting web server to deploy social applications on small machines. It provides online communication tools respecting your privacy and data ownership. You can use Freedom-Box at home to replace services provided by third-parties mining your life and using your content. Thanks to a very friendly interface, you will be able to deploy on demand applications focusing on confidentiality such as file sharing, shared calendaring, instant messaging, secure voice conference calling, blog and wiki. FreedomBox is a free software stack, a subset of the Debian universal operating system, that can be installed in many flavors of inexpensive and power-efficient Open Source hardware, called single board computers (SBC). Once installed on the hardware of your choice, the simplicity of setting up and operating a FreedomBox is similar to that of a smart phone.

SBB License	GNU General Public License (GPL) 2.0
Core Technology	C
Project URL	https://wiki.debian.org/FreedomBox
Source Location	https://wiki.debian.org/FreedomBox/Contribute/Code
Tag(s)	communication, Privacy, VPN

11.0.9 GNUnet

GNUnet is a mesh routing layer for end-to-end encrypted networking and a framework for distributed applications designed to replace the old insecure Internet protocol stack.

In other words, GNUnet provides a strong foundation of free software for a global, distributed network that provides security and privacy. Along with an application for secure publication of files, it has grown to include all kinds of basic applications for the foundation of a GNU internet.

GNUnet is an official GNU package.

The foremost goal of the GNUnet project is to become a widely used, reliable, open, non-discriminating, egalitarian, unfettered and censorship-resistant system of free information exchange. We value free speech above state secrets, law-enforcement or intellectual property. GNUnet is supposed to be an anarchistic network, where the only limitation for peers is that they must contribute enough back to the network such that their resource consumption does not have a significant impact on other users. GNUnet should be more than just another file-sharing network. The plan is to offer many other services and in particular to serve as a development platform for the next generation of decentralized Internet protocols.

SBB License	GNU General Public License (GPL) 2.0
Core Technology	C
Project URL	https://gnunet.org/
Source Location	https://gnunet.org/svn/
Tag(s)	Privacy, Security

11.0.10 IRMA

IRMA offers a privacy-friendly, flexible and secure solution to many authentication problems, putting the user in full control over his/her data.

IRMA contains an app (also OSS), a server and providers. See the site https://privacybydesign.foundation/irma-start/ for more information

The IRMA app manages the user's IRMA attributes: receiving new attributes, selectively disclosing them to others, and attaching them to signed statements. These attributes can be relevant properties, such as: "I am over 18", "my name is ..." and "I am entitled to access ....". They are only stored on the user's device and nowhere else.

SBB License	Apache License 2.0
Core Technology	Java
Project URL	https://privacybydesign.foundation/irma-start/
Source Location	https://github.com/privacybydesign/irma_api_server
Tag(s)	Privacy

11.0.11 Jami

Jami stores your secrets (private keys for encryption and identity) only on the device which executes it, which belongs to you. Your device is therefore the sole holder of your information.

SBB License	GNU General Public License (GPL) 3.0
Core Technology	CPP
Project URL	https://jami.net/
Source Location	https://git.ring.cx/savoirfairelinux/ring-project
Tag(s)	communication, Privacy

11.0.12 MAT: Metadata Anonymisation Toolkit

MAT is a toolbox composed of a GUI application, a CLI application and a library, to anonymize/remove metadata.

Metadata within a file can tell a lot about you. Cameras record data about when and where a picture was taken and what camera was used. Office documents like pdf or Office automatically add author and company information to documents and spreadsheets. Maybe you don't want to disclose this information on the web.

Mat only removes metadata from your files, it does not anonymise their content, nor handle watermarking, steganography, or any overly customized metadata field/system. Also please not that MAT does its best to scrub as much metadata as possible, it's not really efficient at scrubbing embedded media inside complex formats. For examples, images embedded inside PDF may not be cleaned!

SBB License	GNU General Public License (GPL) 3.0
Core Technology	Python
Project URL	https://mat.boum.org/
Source Location	https://gitweb.torproject.org/user/jvoisin/mat.git
Tag(s)	Privacy

11.0.13 Matrix

Matrix is an ambitious new ecosystem for open federated Instant Messaging and VoIP. The basics you need to know to get up and running are:

* Everything in Matrix happens in a room. Rooms are distributed and do not exist on any single server. Rooms can be located using convenience aliases like #matrix:matrix.org or #test:localhost:8448.

* Matrix user IDs look like @matthew:matrix.org (although in the future you will normally refer to yourself and others using a third party identifier (3PID): email address, phone number, etc rather than manipulating Matrix user IDs)

The overall architecture is:

```
client <----> homeserver <=====================>␣
↪homeserver <----> client
      https://somewhere.org/_matrix      https://
↪elsewhere.net/_matrix
```

SBB License	Apache License 2.0
Core Technology	Python
Project URL	https://matrix.org/blog/home/
Source Location	https://github.com/matrix-org/synapse
Tag(s)	communication, Privacy

11.0.14 Mitmproxy

An interactive SSL-capable intercepting HTTP proxy for penetration testers and software developers. Console program that allows traffic flows to be intercepted, inspected, modified and replayed.

Part of mitmproxy is **mitmdump** is the command-line companion to mitmproxy. It provides tcpdump-like functionality to let you view, record, and programmatically transform HTTP traffic. See the `--help` flag output for complete documentation.

SBB License	MIT License
Core Technology	Python
Project URL	https://mitmproxy.org
Source Location	https://github.com/mitmproxy/mitmproxy
Tag(s)	HTTP Proxy, Privacy, Security, Sniffer

11.0.15 Open Whisper (Signal)

Signal is a messaging app for simple private communication with friends. Signal uses your phone's data connection (WiFi/3G/4G) to communicate securely, optionally supports plain SMS/MMS to function as a unified messenger, and can also encrypt the stored messages on your phone.

A private messenger for Android and IOS. Used by Clinton team nowadays.

Private messaging For iPhone and Android. Features:

- Say Anything – Send high-quality group, text, picture, and video messages, all without SMS and MMS fees.

- Be Yourself – Use your existing phone number and address book. There are no separate logins, usernames, passwords, or PINs to manage or lose.

- Stay Private – We cannot read your messages, and no one else can either. Everything is always end-to-end encrypted and painstakingly engineered in order to keep your communication safe.

- Pay Nothing – The development team is supported by community donations and grants. There are no advertisements, and it doesn't cost anything to use.

Note: Some famous hackers have serious doubt on the privacy and especially NSA involvement with Signal. There alternatives like Matrix or Tox that are distributed and can never be compromised!

SBB License	GNU General Public License (GPL) 3.0
Core Technology	Objective C
Project URL	https://whispersystems.org/
Source Location	https://github.com/whispersystems?page=1
Tag(s)	communication, Privacy

11.0.16 PrivacyScore

PrivacyScore is a platform for investigating security and privacy issues on websites. It is inspired by tools like the Qualys SSL test and Webbkoll, but aims to be more comprehensive and offer additional features like

- Comparing and ranking whole lists of sites

- Checking for embedded third parties that are known trackers

- Periodically rescanning each website and checking how the results change over time

- Be completely open source (GPLv3) and easily extendable

SBB License	GNU General Public License (GPL) 3.0
Core Technology	Python
Project URL	https://privacyscore.org/
Source Location	https://github.com/PrivacyScore/PrivacyScore
Tag(s)	Privacy

11.0.17 Searx

Search without being tracked. Searx is a free internet metasearch engine which aggregates results from more than 70 search services. Users are neither tracked nor profiled. Additionally, searx can be used over Tor for online anonymity.

Features:

- Self hosted

- No user tracking

- No user profiling

- About 70 supported search engines

- Easy integration with any search engine

- Cookies are not used by default

- Secure, encrypted connections (HTTPS/SSL)

SBB License	GNU Affero General Public License Version 3
Core Technology	Python
Project URL	https://asciimoo.github.io/searx/
Source Location	https://github.com/asciimoo/searx
Tag(s)	Privacy, Search

11.0.18 Steghide

Steghide is a steganography program that is able to hide data in various kinds of image- and audio-files. The color- respectivly sample-frequencies are not changed thus making the embedding resistant against first-order statistical tests.

Features:

- compression of embedded data

- encryption of embedded data

- embedding of a checksum to verify the integrity of the extraced data

- support for JPEG, BMP, WAV and AU files

Steganography literally means covered writing. Its goal is to hide the fact that communication is taking place. This is often achieved by using a (rather large) cover file and embedding the (rather short) secret message into this file. The result is a innocuous looking file (the stego file) that contains the secret message.

SBB License	GNU General Public License (GPL) 2.0
Core Technology	CPP
Project URL	https://github.com/StefanoDeVuono/steghide
Source Location	https://github.com/StefanoDeVuono/steghide
Tag(s)	Privacy

11.0.19 Streisand

Streisand is software for setting up secure connections with your friends. A bit like TOR.

Streisand is open source software that sets up a communication server that can run:

- WireGuard

- OpenConnect

- OpenSSH

- OpenVPN

- Shadowsocks

- SSHLH

- Stunnel, or a

- Tor bridge.

After configuration Streisand generates custom instructions to use the communication service chosen. At the end of the run you are given an HTML file with instructions that can be shared with friends, family members, and fellow activists. Setting up Streisand requires still some good Unix knowledge for installation and configuration. So it is a bit of a hassle. (status 2018)

Using Streisand reduces the barrier of entry to running a VPN/censorship-bypass server for friends and family and makes secure communication available to more people.

SBB License	GNU General Public License (GPL) 3.0
Core Technology	Python
Project URL	https://github.com/jlund/streisand
Source Location	https://github.com/jlund/streisand
Tag(s)	communication, Privacy, Security

11.0.20 Tails

Tails is a (Debian based) operating system, that you can start on almost any computer from a DVD, USB stick, or SD card. It aims at preserving your privacy and anonymity, and helps you to:

- use the Internet anonymously and circumvent censorship;

- all connections to the Internet are forced to go through the Tor network;

- leave no trace on the computer you are using unless you ask it explicitly;

- use state-of-the-art cryptographic tools to encrypt your files, emails and instant messaging.

SBB License	GNU General Public License (GPL) 2.0
Core Technology	C
Project URL	https://tails.boum.org
Source Location	https://git-tails.immerda.ch/tails/
Tag(s)	Operating System, Privacy

11.0.21 Tor

Tor is free software and an open network that helps you defend against traffic analysis, a form of network surveillance that threatens personal freedom and privacy, confidential business activities and relationships, and state security. Creating your own Tor network is easy with this software, or use existing Tor nodes.

Individuals use Tor to keep websites from tracking them and their family members, or to connect to news sites, instant messaging services, or the like when these are blocked by their local Internet providers. Using Tor protects you against a common form of Internet surveillance known as "traffic analysis." Traffic analysis can be used to infer who is talking to whom over a public network. Knowing the source and destination of your Internet traffic allows others to track your behavior and interests.

Tor is by far the most secure way to enter the internet without giving away your privacy. Thank you Roger Dingledine!

SBB License	GNU General Public License (GPL) 2.0
Core Technology	
Project URL	https://www.torproject.org
Source Location	https://www.torproject.org/dist/
Tag(s)	Cryptography, Privacy, Security

11.0.22 Tox

Whether it's corporations or governments, digital surveillance today is widespread. Tox is easy-to-use software that connects you with friends and family without anyone else listening in. While other big-name services require you to pay for features, Tox is completely free and comes without advertising — forever.

Tox is a peer to peer (serverless) instant messenger aimed at making security and privacy easy to obtain for regular users. It uses NaCl for its encryption and authentication.

SBB License	GNU General Public License (GPL) 3.0
Core Technology	C
Project URL	https://tox.chat/
Source Location	https://github.com/TokTok/c-toxcore
Tag(s)	communication, Privacy

11.0.23 Tribler

Privacy enhanced BitTorrent client with P2P content discovery.

The aim of Tribler is giving anonymous access to online (streaming) videos. We are trying to make privacy, strong cryptography and authentication the Internet norm.

Tribler currently offers a Youtube-style service. For instance, Bittorrent-compatible streaming, fast search, thumbnail previews and comments. For the past 9 years we have been building a very robust Peer-to-Peer system. Today Tribler is robust: "the only way to take Tribler down is to take The Internet down" (but a single software bug could end everything).

Over 2 million people have used Tribler over the years. The Tribler project was started in 2005 at Delft University of Technology and over 100+ developers contributed code to it.

SBB License	GNU General Public License (GPL) 3.0
Core Technology	Python
Project URL	https://www.tribler.org/
Source Location	https://github.com/Tribler/tribler
Tag(s)	communication, Network, Privacy

11.0.24 WireGuard

WireGuard is an extremely simple yet fast and modern VPN that utilizes state-of-the-art cryptography. It aims to be faster, simpler, leaner, and more useful than IPSec, while avoiding the massive headache. It intends to be considerably more performant than OpenVPN. WireGuard is designed as a general purpose VPN for running on embedded interfaces and super computers alike, fit for many different circumstances. Initially released for the Linux kernel, it plans to be cross-platform and widely deployable. It is currently under heavy development, but already it might be regarded as the most secure, easiest to use, and simplest VPN solution in the industry.

SBB License	GNU General Public License (GPL) 2.0
Core Technology	C
Project URL	https://www.wireguard.com/
Source Location	https://git.zx2c4.com/WireGuard/
Tag(s)	Privacy, Security, VPN

11.0.25 XPIR

XPIR: Private Information Retrieval for Everyone

XPIR allows a user to privately download an element from a database. This means that the database server knows that she has sent a database element to the user but does not know which one. The scientific term for the underlying protocol is Private Information Retrieval (PIR). This library is described and studied in the paper:

Carlos Aguilar-Melchor, Joris Barrier, Laurent Fousse, Marc-Olivier Killijian, "XPIR: Private Information Retrieval for Everyone", Proceedings on Privacy Enhancing Technologies. Volume 2016, Issue 2, Pages 155–174, ISSN (Online) 2299-0984, DOI: 10.1515/popets-2016-0010, December 2015.

SBB License	GNU General Public License (GPL) 3.0
Core Technology	C
Project URL	' <> '__
Source Location	https://github.com/XPIR-team/XPIR
Tag(s)	Network, Privacy

End of SBB list

Chapter 11. OSS Privacy Applications

TWELVE

OPEN TOOLBOX

Besides software tools many tools within the field of security and privacy are knowlegde tools. Valuable design templates, risk sheets or collections of models that will help creating your solution.

When creating this reference architecture, we performed serious research. We used many valuable sources (books, articles, scientific publications, blogs, etc). In this section you will find real reusable tools. All tools are focused on helping to solve your security and/or privacy challenge easier. So you will find many reusable real open (cc-by) tools for so you can create your solution without reinventing the wheel again.

We believe that all knowledge for building better security and privacy solutions should be available under an open access license. This is why all references in this section are open access references or available for free under an open liberal license.

12.0.1 Secure Coding Guidelines

Securing coding is the practice of developing software that prevents security and privacy risks. Coding defects, bugs and logic flaws are a main cause of many software vulnerabilities. Since prevention is better than less complex than fixing security defects later, every software engineer should use Secure Coding guidelines and practices.

12.0.2 Reproducible builds

Reproducible builds are a set of software development practices that create an independently-verifiable path from source code to the binary code used by computers. Reproducible Builds project gives rules, guidelines, tools and more to allow verification that no vulnerabilities or backdoors have been introduced during the software compilation process.

https://reproducible-builds.org/

12.0.3 Mozilla

Mozilla is an OSS Foundation that produces a Browser and various other online communication tools. Security and privacy is a number one priority for the Mozilla Foundation. Mozilla produces large amount of code in various programming languages. One of the secure coding guidelines that is used internal can be found here: https://wiki.mozilla.org/WebAppSec/Secure_Coding_Guidelines

12.0.4 GOlang programming

Go Language Web Application Secure Coding Practices, https://checkmarx.gitbooks.io/go-scp/ CC-Licensed so you can edit this Git-Book yourself. Check the repository on https://github.com/Checkmarx/Go-SCP And of course OWASP Secure Coding Practices are used for this GO specific publication.

12.0.5 OSS Security Software Repositories

The NSA Technology Transfer Program (TTP) works with agency innovators who wish to use this collaborative model for transferring their technology to the commercial marketplace. OSS invites cooperative development of technology, encouraging broad use and adoption.

The collection of NSA repositories is large and some are too good to be neglected. To name a few:

- Apache Accumulo: A sorted, distributed key/value store that provides robust, scalable data storage and retrieval. It adds cell-based access control and a server-side programming mechanism that can modify key/value pairs at various points in the data management process.

- CASA: Identifies unexpected and prohibited Certificate Authority certificates on Windows systems.

- DCP: A program that reduces the timespan needed for making a forensic copy of hard drives for forensic analysis.

- JAVA PATHFINDER MANGO (JPF-MANGO): A static code analysis tool that uses formal methods for analysis. It is part of NASA Ames Java PathFinder project which is a system used to verify executable Java byte code.

- LEMONGRAPH/LEMONGRENADE:Log-based transactional graph database engine backed by a single file. The primary use case is to support streaming seed set expansion, iterative correlation, and recursive file processing.

- Apache NIFI: Automates the flow of data between systems. NiFi implements concepts of Flow-Based Programming and solves common data flow problems faced by enterprises.

- OPENATTESTATION:Verifies system integrity by establishing a baseline measurement of a system's Trusted Platform Module (TPM) and monitors for changes in that measurement. Originally based on NSA's Host Integrity at Startup (HIS) software.

- SYSTEM INTEGRITY MANAGEMENT PLATFORM (SIMP):Automates system configuration and compliance of Linux operating systems so they conform to industry best practices.

For all NSA repositories see: https://nationalsecurityagency.github.io/

12.0.6 General information on information security

High-level overview of information security principles: https://nvlpubs.nist.gov/nistpubs/SpecialPublications/NIST.SP.800-12r1.pdf

Software Security Knowledge Area: https://www.cybok.org/news/software-security-ka-issue-10 Document of the CyBOK project(https://www.cybok.org) to harvest security knowledge.

Cryptography KA issue 1.0, 2018:https://www.cybok.org/news/cryptography-ka-issue-10 Also of the CyBok project.

12.0.7 Attacks methods

Rowhammer: http://www.thirdio.com/rowhammer.pdf or https://en.wikipedia.org/wiki/Row_hammer

DDos: https://www.us-cert.gov/sites/default/files/publications/DDoS%20Quick%20Guide.pdf

12.0.8 Thread Models

The OWASP Automated Threat Handbook provides actionable information and resources to help defend against automated threats to web applications. https://www.owasp.org/images/3/33/Automated-threat-handbook.pdf

12.0.9 Security Frameworks

NIST Framework for Improving Critical Infrastructure Cybersecurity:

http://www.nist.gov/cyberframework/upload/cybersecurity-framework-021214.pdf

http://www.nist.gov/cyberframework/

Jericho security model, Open Group, https://collaboration.opengroup.org/jericho/

NIST, http://www.nist.gov/cyberframework/index.cfm

OECD privacy framework 2009, 2010,http://oecdprivacy.org/

Software Assurance Maturity Model (OWASP), http://www.opensamm.org/

Open Security Architecture (OSA), http://www.opensecurityarchitecture.org/

Mozilla Information Security Guides, https://infosec.mozilla.org/ Technical guidelines, principles and general information as used by the infosec team of Mozilla.

12.0.10 Privacy References Architectures and Models

Privacy represents a broad variety of concerns — subjective, contextual, hard-to-define — that real people have about the flows of personal information. This initiative is building a living, community space where everyone can contribute their privacy design patterns. https://privacypatterns.org

IMMA Privacy reference architecture, publication of the Dutch Ministry of Infrastructure and the Environment,March 2016, http://www.beterbenutten.nl/assets/upload/files/IMMA/IMMA-Privacy-reference-architecture-EN-2016.pdf

Privacy Management Reference Model and Methodology (PMRM) Version 1.0, Committee Specification Draft 01, 26 March 2012, http://docs.oasis-open.org/pmrm/PMRM/v1.0/csd01/PMRM-v1.0-csd01.pdf

Privacy Management Reference Model and Methodology (PMRM) Version 1.0, http://docs.oasis-open.org/pmrm/PMRM/v1.0/csd01/PMRM-v1.0-csd01.html

AICPA/CICA Privacy Maturity Model March 2011, http://www.aicpa.org/InterestAreas/InformationTechnology/Resources/Privacy/GenerallyAcceptedPrivacyPrinciples/DownloadableDocuments/AICPA-CICA-Privacy-Maturity-Model-ebook.pdf

Generally Accepted Privacy Principles (GAPP),https://www.cippguide.org/2010/07/01/generally-accepted-privacy-principles-gapp/

12.0.11 Open Access Privacy Journals

Proceedings on Privacy Enhancing Technologies http://www.degruyter.com/view/j/popets

PoPETs is the journal that publishes papers accepted to the Privacy Enhancing Technologies Symposium (PETS). PETS brings together privacy and anonymity experts from around the world to discuss recent advances and new perspectives. PETS addresses the design and realization of privacy services for the Internet and other data systems and communication networks.

12.0.12 Transactions on Data Privacy

The aim of the Transactions on Data Privacy (TDP) is to provide an international forum for researchers on all topics related to data privacy technologies. http://www.tdp.cat/

12.0.13 Guide to data protection

This guide is for those who have day-to-day responsibility for data protection. It explains the purpose and effect of each principle, gives practical examples and answers frequently asked questions. https://ico.org.uk/for-organisations/guide-to-data-protection/

12.0.14 Open Foundations on security & Privacy

Python Forensics, Inc.

A non-profit organization focused on the collaborative development of open source investigative technologies using the Python programming language. See: http://python-forensics.org/ for more information.

OpenSCAP

The OpenSCAP project provides tools to improve security of your infrastructure using open source tools. This project is founded by RedHat and the tools are NIST certified. Use of the tools is encouraged if your systems or infrastructure needs to meet NIST (or other US) security standards. https://www.open-scap.org/

Center for Internet Security (CIS)

The Center for Internet Security (CIS) is a 501(c)(3) organization is dedicated to enhancing the cybersecurity readiness and response among public and private sector entities. CIS's Mission is to: Identify, develop, validate, promote, and sustain best practices in cybersecurity; Deliver world-class security solutions to prevent and rapidly respond to cyber incidents; and Build and lead communities to enable an environment of trust in cyberspace. https://www.cisecurity.org/

No-More-Ransom

The "No-More-Ransom" website is an initiative by the National High Tech Crime Unit of the Netherlands' police, Europol's European Cybercrime Centre and two cyber security companies – Kaspersky Lab and Intel Security – with the goal to help victims of ransomware retrieve their encrypted data without having to pay the criminals. https://www.nomoreransom.org/

Open State Foundation

A Dutch foundation fighting for more digital transparency in the Netherlands. http://www.openstate.eu/

Security in-a-box

Security in-a-Box is a guide to digital security for activists and human rights defenders throughout the world. Security in-a-box offers a guide and real nice tools for everyone who cares about privacy in a volatile world. See https://securityinabox.org/en

Privacytools.io

Privacytools.io is a socially motivated website that provides information for protecting your data security and privacy. The site has an impressive tool collection https://www.privacytools.io/ Yes, we can not incorporate all tools in this reference architecture. Our list is opinionated to surprise you only with some great examples to make you hungry!

SOMAP.org

Focuses on the Security Officers and on helping them in doing their daily business as comfortable as possible. The main goals of SOMAP.org are to develop and maintain: - Guides and Handbooks explaining and describing Risk Management. - an open and free 'best practice' Risk Model Repository with security objectives, threats and other risk related metadata. https://www.somap.org/

Data Transparency Lab (DTL)

A community of technologists, researchers, policymakers and industry representatives working to advance online personal data transparency through scientific research and design. Also a collection of OSS tools to visualize internet privacy horror are offered. http://www.datatransparencylab.org

P=P Foundation = Privacy by Default

The P=P foundation advocates Privacy. The p-p engine was developed for this purpose and drives several crypto standards on different digital channels. It shall ultimately restore Privacy by Default. p-p engine is distributed as Free Software to support Privacy for everyone. With that p-p aims to restore the balance again in worldwide communications in favor of Privacy and Freedom of Information. https://pep.foundation/index.html

ICO

The ICO is the UK's independent body set up to uphold information rights. The UK's independent authority set up to uphold information rights in the public interest, promoting openness by public bodies and data privacy for individuals. https://ico.org.uk/

12.0.15 Checklists

The list with security and privacy checklists is long. However in this opinionated list we collected OPEN lists (so under an open license published) that are ready to use and to improve. OSS Security Badges project (Work in progress), D. Wheeler, https://github.com/linuxfoundation/cii-best-practices-badge/blob/master/criteria.md

Linux workstation security checklist: https://github.com/lfit/itpol/blob/master/linux-workstation-security.md

Guide to securing personal information (Australian government): https://www.oaic.gov.au/agencies-and-organisations/guides/guide-to-securing-personal-information

Securing Web Application Technologies [SWAT] Checklist: https://
software-security.sans.org/resources/swat

Kubernetes Security- Best Practice Guide, https://github.com/freach/
kubernetes-security-best-practice

REST API Checklist: Summary of important security countermeasures
when designing, testing, and releasing your API, https://github.com/
shieldfy/API-Security-Checklist

12.0.16 Vulnerability Databases

Common Weakness Enumeration (CWE™), cwe.mitre.org

12.0.17 Learning and training resources

The wargames offered by the OverTheWire community can help you
to learn and practice security concepts in the form of fun-filled games.
All OSS with the code on Github. Check it out: http://overthewire.org/
wargames/

Key Reinstallation Attacks- Breaking WPA2 by forcing nonce reuse
(KRACK). With hands-on description, check it out: https://www.
krackattacks.com/

Practical Cryptography for Developers: https://cryptobook.nakov.com/

12.0.18 Open Source Initiative (OSI)

To learn more about the Open source licenses and the foundation behind
this initiative: The Open Source Initiative (OSI), http://opensource.org/
licenses/

12.0.19 Libre Router project

The Libre Router project is creating a high performance multi-radio wireless router targeted at Community Networks needs. So if you are keen
on privacy, check https://librerouter.org/home

12.0.20 Information Security Guide

Guide setup like this one, so to prevent to reinvent the wheel every time you start a new project, policy, or security function. https://spaces. internet2.edu/display/2014infosecurityguide/Welcome+to+the+Guide

The Free Software Foundation, https://www.gnu.org

Web Authorization Protocol (OAuth), https://tools.ietf.org/html/ draft-ietf-oauth-v2-threatmodel-01

THIRTEEN

ABOUT THE AUTHORS

This first release of the open reference architecture for security and privacy is created by the following IT security architects:

13.0.1 Asim Jahan

Asim works as an information security and privacy consultant. As such he likes to improve or redesign business processes enabling companies and organisations to perform better with less effort at less costs. He holds a Bachelor degree in Business IT & Management of The Hague University. Asim knows the GDPR inside out. He also has all knowledge of CIPP/E and CIPM. He currently works for the government implementing GDPR together with a handpicked team. He likes to speak and recently Asim joined a debating club. blogs and observes developments in cyber realms. Take a look at his LinkedIn profile: https://nl.linkedin.com/in/asimjahan.

13.0.2 Maikel Mardjan

Maikel works often as IT (security) architect and loves to make designs for complex IT systems in a simple way. Maikel holds both a Master (Msc) Business Studies of University of Groningen and a Master degree (Msc) Electrical Engineering, of Delft University of Technology. Maikel is TOGAF 9 Certified and CISSP (Certified Information Systems Security Professional) certified. Maikel currently works for the innovative IT company nocomplexity.com. Despite privacy concerns, Maikel can be found on Twitter too https://twitter.com/maikelmardjan

Chapter 13. About the authors

FOURTEEN

LICENSING

Thank you for downloading or buying this book. We want people to reuse content of this reference architecture in their own security solution architectures or privacy solution architectures. Security is hard enough, so reuse good open solutions available today. If you like to reuse text of this reference architecture in your own work: presentations, articles or your own book you are free to do so under the conditions that belong to the Creative Commons cc-by-sa license.

We have chosen to use the cc-by-sa license so this reference architecture is created to be shared as much as possible. Also using the cc-by-sa license lowers barriers for creating a better version of this reference architecture.

This work is licensed under a Creative Commons Attribution-ShareAlike 4.0 International License. See http://creativecommons.org/licenses/by-sa/4.0/ for the full license text or here below:

You are free to:

- Share — copy and redistribute the material in any medium or format

- Adapt — remix, transform, and build upon the material for any purpose, even commercially.

The licensor cannot revoke these freedoms as long as you follow the license terms.

Under the following terms:

- Attribution — You must give appropriate credit, provide a link to the license, and indicate if changes were made. You may do so in any reasonable manner, but not in any way that suggests the licensor endorses you or your use.

- ShareAlike — If you remix, transform, or build upon the material, you must distribute your contributions under the same license as the original.

No additional restrictions — You may not apply legal terms or technological measures that legally restrict others from doing anything the license permits.

Notices:

- You do not have to comply with the license for elements of the material in the public domain or where your use is permitted by an applicable exception or limitation.

- No warranties are given. The license may not give you all of the permissions necessary for your intended use. For example, other rights such as publicity, privacy, or moral rights may limit how you use the material.

FIFTEEN

CONTRIBUTING

We encourage all security professionals to improve this reference architecture. Join the team to:

- Add security or privacy principles.

- Add security or privacy models.

- Help us create the largest OSS reference framework on OSS security and privacy applications and tools.

- Create better graphics and text.

- Add threat models that can be easily reused.

- Improve criteria on selecting OSS solutions for security and privacy applications.

Your contributions to this Guide are greatly appreciated as long as contributions fit within the scope and goal of this security and privacy reference architecture. As an open project, this Open Reference Architecture for Security and Privacy shall always remain vendor-neutral and freely available for all to use. If you contribute you will of course get credit (mentioned in upcoming publications).

You can contribute using the following Github repository:
https://github.com/nocomplexity/SecurityPrivacyReferenceArchitecture

Please observe our contribution guidelines before creating a pull request:

With the exception of typos and spelling mistakes (feel free to fix these and they'll be merged), please take notice of the following guidelines:

- Always open an issue first. This will allow us to determine whether or not the change should take place. Explain your issue, and we will discuss it with you. If we agree the change is necessary we will mark it as TODO and will fix it when we get a chance, or we will allow a member of the community to supply the change with a pull request.

- Note that this reference architecture is intended to be a helpful resource aimed at professional security/privacy architects and designers.

- Contributions must fit within the scope and goal of this security and privacy reference architecture. Of course we like to discuss your input for changing scope or goals if needed!

Please follow the following procedure when contributing to this document:

- Fork the chapter you want to change or contribute on GitHub, with the Fork button

- Clone the repository to your computer

- Create a branch in which you make your patch git checkout -b <branchname>

- Make your changes, commit and push the branch

- – edit, edit, edit
  - git add files, git commit
  - git push origin <branchname>

- Create a pull request for the branch <branchname> you created (not 'master')

Since we know many security professionals are not familiar with GitHub, we are currently investigating other methods to lower barriers for contributing to this project.

The maintainers review your pull request and your patch is merged with the master branch ASAP.

Licensing

When you submit text to which you hold the copyright, you agree to license it under:

- Creative Commons Attribution-ShareAlike 4.0 International License ("CC BY-SA")

Printed in Great Britain
by Amazon